Management Models for the Future

Jan Jonker · Jacob Eskildsen (Eds.)

Management Models
for the Future

Editors

Prof. Dr. Jan Jonker
Radbound University Nijmegen
Nijmegen School of Management
PO BOX 9108
6500 HK Nijmegen
The Netherlands
janjonker@wxs.nl

Dr. Jacob Eskildsen
Aarhus Business School
Haslegardsvej 10
8210 Aarhus V
Denmark
eskildsen@asb.dk

ISBN 978-3-540-71450-7   e-ISBN 978-3-540-71451-4

DOI 10.1007/978-3-540-71451-4

Library of Congress Control Number: 2009920214

Cover design: WMXDesign GmbH, Heidelberg

Printed on acid-free paper

9 8 7 6 5 4 3 2 1

springer.com

Table of Contents

Management Models for the Future

A brief explorative inquiry into the "raison d'être" of management models

Jacob Eskildsen, Jan Jonker, and Michel van Pijkeren

Abstract. In light of a growing number of management models used in organisations questions regarding their nature, validity and applicability are becoming more and more important. We therefore provide in this introduction a concise overview of their background. We define a management model as: a "stable" theoretical framework that can be used to observe, create and assess a real life organizational 'situation' in order to make desired (future) improvements. We also argue that five common requirements can be used to appraise the applicability of a framework claiming to be a management model. Thereafter a brief outline will be provided of each of the twelve business contributions in this volume. The experiences recorded in the following chapters are wide-ranging. They cover know-how with national quality award models; management models for fair trade, corporate social responsibility, organisational excellence and various aspects of an organisations' value chain. The volume makes available an intriguing journey into the application of management models in different organizational and environmental contexts – a great learning experience for anyone who undertakes it.

Key words: Management Models, theoretical framework, applicability.

1 Introduction

More than 500 years a go, in 1494, Luco Bartolemeo Pacioli, a Franciscan friar and a gifted mathematician, became the first person to describe double-entry accounting, also known as the Venetian Method, in his famous book *"Summa de arithmetica, geometria, proportioni et proportionalita"*. This then new system was state-of-the-art, and revolutionized economy and business of that time as well as immortalized Pacioli as the "Farther of Accounting". Since then five centuries have gone bye. Since then the industrial revolution gave birth to the business enterprise. Since about half a century we are witnessing the birth of a service or 'experience' economy where intangible aspects are dominating the tangibles. In recent years we have witnessed the start of what might turn out to be the downfall of traditional approach to running an organisation. Today the accounting system tells investors less and less about the actual value and values of a company exemplified by the book to market value ratio which is steadily increasing, especially for companies belonging to the new economy. Intangible aspects such as reputation, image, contribution to the broader society etc. seem to put more and more weight in assessing the value of a company. Many companies struggle with the question how to design and organise these new and – often difficult to grasp – demands. While roots of the contemporary organisation can be found in a bygone industrial area, the present market and societal demands are such that new designs and new concepts are imminent. No wonder many organisations are in need of renovation, innovation and reinvigoration.

If Pacioli's established approach to organising the business proposition were all still working effectively then the contemporary business would not offer so many examples of failure, scandals, discontinuity, continuous struggle with change and lack of 'fit' with markets and consumers. Some companies are addressing these challenges, many companies however don't. New functional requirements often seem in opposition to each other. Trying to handle transparency, stock market performance, sustainability, innovation, responsibility, time to market, a growing array of stakeholders, business rationalisation and many other issues and demands all at the same time is for sure not an easy task. No wonder many managers – mentally equipped with organisational knowledge from a different area – struggle with question 'how' to realise this transition. Whatever will happen, all signs point in the direction of reinforcing revision of designs and concepts and realignment with novel needs and expectations inside and outside the organisation. Fundamental strategic choices have to be made in that regard. A 'one strategy fits all' approach is outdated if not dangerous. Instead a multi-layer strategy map requesting internal en external alignment seems the way to go. It is clear that the time is right to re-conceptualise the business enterprise.

In a spontaneous attempt to address these issues recent years a rapidly growing number of management models (e.g. EFQM, INK, ISO 9000:2000, SA 8000, AA 1000, GRI, QRES, Six Sigma, Balanced Score Cards etc.) has evolved. Somehow they all stipulate to describe the road to excellent organisational performance. A recent study in Denmark for example has shown that approximately 47% of all Danish companies is using some sort of management model (Kristensen & Eskildsen 2006). ISO 9001:2000 is now firmly established as the globally accepted standard for providing assurance about the quality of goods and services in supplier-customer relations. Up to the end of December 2005, at least 776,608 ISO 9001:2000 certificates had been issued in 161 countries and economies, an increase of 18 % over 2004, when the total was 660,132 in 154 countries and economies. Similarly, ISO 14001 confirms its global relevance for organizations wishing to operate in an environmentally sustainable manner. Up to the end of December 2005, at least 111,162 ISO 14001 certificates (1996 and 2004 versions consolidated) had been issued in 138 countries and economies, an increase of 24 % over 2004, when the total was 89,937 in 127 countries and economies (source: http://www.iso.org, May 2007)

The underlying claim is that if companies apply one of these models they should – ceteris paribus – reach a higher level of performance and excellence than they otherwise would have been able to achieve. The term management model describes a broad range of informal and formal models that are used by organisations to represent various (functional, social and emotional) aspects of a business, such as operational processes, organisational structures, and financial forecasts. Although the term can be traced to the 1950s, it achieved mainstream usage only in the 1990s. Many informal definitions of the term can be found in popular business literature. For example: "A business model is a conceptual tool that contains a big set of elements and their relationships and allows expressing the business logic of a specific firm. It is a description of the value a company offers to one or several segments of customers and of the architecture of the firm and its network of partners for creating, marketing, and delivering this value and relationship capital, to generate profitable and sustainable revenue streams." (Osterwalder, Pigneur and Tucci , 2005).

A confusion related to the business model concept is that many people speak about business models when they really only mean parts of a business model [Linder and Cantrell 2000]. What also raises confusion is the maxim that many models are useful in various situations – in whole or in part. This is also known as the 'contingency theory'. In essence this implies that a management style and organizational structure are influenced by various aspects of the environment: the contingency factors. There is not "one best way" for leadership or the design of the organization. Usability depends on the context and providing guidance for managers in relation to creating desired improvements. All this off course raises the question of the applicability of these management models. The aim of this introductory chapter is therefore to highlight the "raison d'être" of management models as well as to outline some general requirements that frameworks must fulfil if they are to be truly management models.

2   The "raison d'être" of management models

Existence of organisations is based upon the production of outcomes such as "profit", "common goods" or the production of ideologies. Outcome should by definition create value; outcome that can only be achieved while respecting the wellbeing of organisational members and taking into account its 'environment' [the community and its customers] relevant for its existence (Jonker & Eskildsen, 2002). Organisations thus don't exist because they are making profit; profit is a reward for creating value. The organisation as such is 'the instrument' to achieve that outcome. The actual realisation of this outcome can only come about in interaction with the context [or environment] in which the organisation operates. To make a profit is based upon the fact that people buy products or services. The definition of appropriate products and services change continuously over time and making the right choices at a given moment to fulfil the needs and expectations of people [be it employees, customers, suppliers, stockholders or society at large] can be done in a variety of ways. This is referred to as 'contingency' or 'equifinality' (Jonker & Eskildsen, 2002).

More and more people in industry also realises that a company's condition cannot be summarised merely by a financial analysis. If operational improvements are made the financial measures will automatically follow. So there is a need for ways to measure and analyse the company's ability to make operational improvements. This has made many organisations search for alternative measures and models of performance. Currently there exist a smorgasbord of organisational models that describes various aspects of organisational performance.

A model is by definition a representation of something else, something that is not – or cannot be – present or is not tangible. It is "a set of basic assumptions or fundamental principles of intellectual origin from which discussion and actions can proceed" (Popper, 1994). It should create a certain order from observable and measurable facts that might appear at first hand chaotic and unrelated. Here the focus is on models regarding organisations either as a whole or focussing on a specific function [e.g. quality or corporate social responsibility]. The first are often called 'holistic' models, the latter 'functional' or 'function specific' models.

A management model provides a "stable" theoretical framework that can be used to observe, create and assess a real life organisational 'situation' in order to make desired (future) improvements (Eskildsen & Jonker, 2001; Rüegg-Stürm, 2005). As a whole a model offers [implicit] research methods and standards to make a comparison between the present and future possibilities through an organisational self-assessment. In that respect it is a tool for comparison – between the present situation and a desired situation in the future – based upon its own values, structure, methodology, methods and techniques. Guillen (1994) argues that in the history of management science three overriding models of management have been developed; (a) scientific management, (b) human relations and (c) structural analysis. Adopting one of the models or using elements of the models in conjunction is dependent on the contextual setting in which the organisation operates. Managers tend to combine elements of the three models given a certain context. In other words: there is not one best way of organising, design or managing.

Management models tend to be complex because they need to address two intertwined issues at the same time: (1) the functional task of organising – what should be done by whom and in what order; and (2) establishing, maintaining and justifying a system of authority. One could call the latter also a 'future perspective' – one that guides the way towards a nearby future. The way in which managers perceive, assess, and interpret problems is partially shaped by some ideology, i.e. a set of assumptions about how the world works and how it ought to work. Management models are in this respect useful to managers because they allow to interpret a problem and provide practical guidelines for action leading towards a desired future (Guillen, 1994). Its possible contribution can thus be "...a contribution ... in the creation of concepts and tools that help manager to capture, understand, communicate, design, analyze, and change the business logic of their firm. As such: "Business models help to capture, visualize, understand, communicate and share the business logic (Osterwalder, Pigneur and Tucci , 2005:19).

2.1 Self-assessment

The use of management models as a means to identify opportunities for improvement and change within organisations is called organisational self-assessment. Self-assessment in an organisational setting refers to a comprehensive, systematic and regular review of an organisations' activities and results referenced against a model. It allows the organisation to discern clearly its strengths and areas in which improvements can be made and culminates in planned improvement actions which are then monitored for progress. Organisational self-assessment is defined as a first-party evaluation that has the following characteristics:

- it is improvement and not conformance oriented;
- it is based on a framework that relates every aspect of the organisations' operations to the performance of the organisation;
- it is a diagnostic tool that can identify internal and external performance gaps by means of systematic approaches;
- it is a tool that initiates improvements actions which are then monitored for progress;
- it is an ongoing and regular activity in the organisation.

The main purpose of organisational self-assessment is to aid the organisational quest for superior or new performance by enabling the identification of the drivers for performance. Research has shown that companies using these frameworks experience a lot of gains from the self-assessment process ranging from increased employee involvement to improved bottom line results. Especially the companies' increased focus on the customer and on continuous improvements has been pointed out as a major benefit from the self-assessment process. Especially management models originating from the quality field (quality award, ISO 9000, balanced scorecard, etc.) have gained increasing attention from companies and there are more than fifty national quality awards and an increasing number of large corporations have implemented quality certification programs for their suppliers.

Some findings also indicate that it makes good financial sense to apply a holistic reporting system. The largest study of this phenomenon was conducted in the US where app. 600 quality award winning companies were followed over a five year period (Hendricks & Singhal, 2001). This group of award winners was then compared to relevant benchmarks such as the S&P 500. This analysis revealed that the award winning companies outperformed the benchmarks and all the financial indicators included in the study (Hendricks & Singhal, 2001). This kind of research however does not support any statistical generalisations concerning the effect of holistic management models in industry at large.

2.2   The case of Denmark

The effect in industry at large has on the other hand been the focus of a Danish study conducted five times from 1998 to 2003. In this longitudinal study approximately 700 CEOs answered a questionnaire related to their companies' use of management models. This information was then linked to actual financial results (Kristensen et all, 2002). The results of this analysis are shown in Figure 1 were control charts for operating profit for users and non-users of

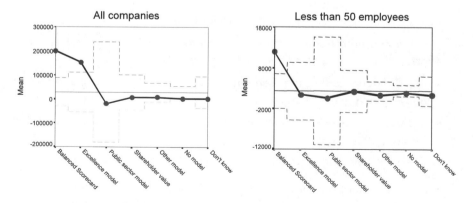

Figure 1. The financial effect of holistic management models

different generic management models are shown for all companies and for companies with less that 50 employees. On the horizontal axis of these charts is the model in question and the average financial result is on the vertical axis. The dotted lines indicate the 2-sigma control limits.

The figure clearly shows that when looking at industry at large there is a clear positive effect of both the Balanced Scorecard and the EFQM Excellence Model, while companies using one of the remaining models do not show any significant effect different from companies that are not using any model at all. Taken strictly this is not a proof that the balanced scorecard and the excellence model actually produce better results than other models. The effects may be confounded with other factors and it will take an experiment to resolve this problem.

Furthermore the figure shows that the EFQM Excellence Model has no financial effect for companies with less than 50 employees. In this case it is only the Balanced Scorecard that shows an effect. Apart from giving an indication to small companies concerning choice of model this also gives an indication that the EFQM SME model is not sufficiently simple for small companies to use. This conclusion is supported by a number of case-studies focusing on the applicability of management models in relation to small and medium-sized companies

The Danish study implies that organisations change their view on the way the organisation operates when they apply a management model. In other words they gain a better understanding of the world they operate in and how they achieve their results. The perceived importance of the "people" dimension of the organisation increases and this might be due to the fact that the organisations that apply a management model have realised the importance of the employees with respect to embarking on continuous improvements. Not only do CEOs of organisations that apply management models put more emphasis on the "people" dimension they also report significant better HR performance than non-users. This HR focus can also be seen in their willingness to apply performance related pay. There is a clear tendency towards the use of performance related pay increases among users of management models so that it to a higher extend includes all employees.

2.3 Application of management models

When talking about management models it is important to remember that they are not a miracle cure in the sense that application will guarantee organisational success. Applying a management model is hard work that requires dedication, persistency and courage but if these three prerequisites are present the desired changes are possible. An organisation may apply a management model for a variety of reasons. It could be with the aim of mapping the value chains of the organisation or because the organisations choose a more structured approach to corporate social responsibility. No matter what the specific motivation may be, the overriding theme is organisational change. The important thing to remember is that the application of a management model will bring about other unforeseen consequences for the organisation.

In this sense management models are tools to guide these processes of choice[s] within organisations. Management models differ from the most common everyday tools – such as hammers, knives or pans – in the sense that they are not physical by nature. They are a systematised whole based upon methodological, methodical and instrumental choices focussing on a particular subject [organisations] of a manageable property [e.g. quality or corporate social responsibility]. They differ also from common tools that they are not an object or "a thing" that can be observed or measured. The "tool" only comes "alive" once a person starts using the model (Jonker & Eskildsen, 2002).

Usage however cannot be a goal in itself. The true measure for the applicability of any management model is whether or not the model can be a used to guide informed decisions about future actions based on a causal model structure. A management model never gives a complete description of an organisation and its context. The whole idea of management models is to provide a condensed version of reality – one by which managing complexity is facilitated. The search for the one true model is thus a futile quest since it does not exist. As the famous quality-guru Deming said: "Every theorem is true in its own world. The question is, which world are we in?".

3   Lessons from the business community

So far we have argued that the history of management science shows three overriding models of management; scientific management, human relations and structural analysis. However the search for alternative measures and models of performance has resulted in a vast variety of organisational models that describe various aspects of organisational performance. Furthermore the process through which management models are applied identifying opportunities for improvement within organisations becomes rather crucial. Companies that apply a management model experience a lot of challenges but also gains ranging from increased employee involvement to improved bottom line results. In the following chapters twelve organisations from around the world operating in totally different markets provide insights into their 'customised' approach in dealing with one or more of these requirements as well as their experiences and benefits of applying their specific management model. These contributions where written by the companies themselves on our request. Based on a strict format they provide a comparable overview of what goes on inside the company. The companies contributing their insights are the following.

3.1 Cilag (Switzerland)

Cilag AG is one of the leading Swiss firms in the pharmaceutical industry. In this chapter the company describes how demands for new and better management support has led to an organisational process whose emergence has been brought about with the help of management models at different levels of the business. The focus is on lessons from creating and implementing innovative management models.

3.2 Henkel (Germany)

Henkel is headquartered in Düsseldorf, Germany and operates in three business areas: Home Care; Personal Care; and Adhesives, Sealants and Surface Treatment in which the company is one of the world leading producers. Henkel's social commitment is firmly embedded in its corporate values and its corporate history and in this chapter the company offers insights from one of the most comprehensive social commitment initiatives.

3.3 Danske Bank (Denmark)

Danske Bank is the leading financial institution in Denmark and one of the largest and highest rated in the Nordic region. Danske Bank has for many years measured and analyzed various aspects of business performance and in this chapter Danske Bank shares some of their insights with respect to mapping the value-chain in a commercial bank. The emphasis is on the relationship between employee satisfaction and motivation on one side and customer loyalty and customer profitability on the other.

3.4 AgroFair

AgroFair applies a business model that might provide an answer for gaining market access for small producer organisations from developing countries. One of the central pillars of the company is the concept of co-ownership in a vertically integrated supply chain. The credentials are embedded in its vision statement of A Fair Price, A Fair Say and a Fair Share. This chapter describes the history of the AgroFair business model and analyzes the crucial elements that have contributed to its success.

3.5 ABN AMRO Real (Brazil)

Since 1998, ABN AMRO Real, the third largest private bank in Brazil, has relentlessly worked to create a 'sounder bank for a sounder society', integrating social, environmental and economic aspects into the business. Its management model dates back to 2001 and is used to guide the organisation towards achieving its ambitious vision and mission. In this chapter ABN AMRO Real demonstrates that the integration of sustainability into its model is a win-win-win strategy for shareholders, clients, employees and other stakeholders.

3.6 Danish Post (Denmark)

In 1998 Post Danmark launched a massive change process based on the TQM philosophy. This entailed systematic measures to steer the organisation away from the traditional government service culture developing it towards a more modern and dynamic organisational culture. This chapter describes the process that lead to Post Danmark winning the Danish Quality Award in 2004 and being a finalist for the European Quality Award in 2006.

3.7 Western Australian Water Cooperation (Australia)

The Water Corporation of Western Australia is a State Government-owned corporatised water utility, which operates over the huge 2.5 million square kilometre land area of Western Australia. The Water Corporation has embarked on a journey of business transformation, with environmental, social and financial sustainability as the prime conceptual and ethical drivers and in this chapter the company describes lessons learned and benefits achieved.

3.8 Triodos Bank (Netherlands)

The Triodos Foundation was founded in 1973 with the aim of financing projects and ventures that had a societal cause. The Triodos Bank was established in 1980 in the Netherlands with the overriding goal to foster societal renewal As an organisation with a clear mission the Triodos Bank is build on human capital and deploys a management model that places the individual at the heart. The Triodos Bank takes up a bridging role between the individual and society at large. It is a place where individuals connect and collaborate to make things done that cannot be made alone.

3.9 Vandemoortele (Germany)

Vandemoortele Deutschland GmbH is part of a Europe wide food manufacturer (margarine, bakery-products, soya-products). The company supplies mainly German food retail chains which are dominated by discounters. In this chapter the company demonstrates that the German system of resolving conflicts of interest through employee participation has not only served the country well during the period of post-war economic growth but also provides the ideal framework for a management model designed to minimize costs and resist fierce competition.

3.10 Gaz de France (France)

Gaz du France, a privatised Frech energy giant is confronted with the challenges of internationalising its operations and sales activities. The effects of rapid internationalisation and the diversification of its activities have meant that Gaz de France had to adapt its managerial practices to its diversified context. The system it has developed to meet these new requirements endeavours to combine respect for diversity with the need for coordination over the company's new scope of activity. It does not impose a single management method but rather proposes common references within which each manager is encouraged to continuously improve his or her practices, thus contributing to the group's sustainable performance.

3.11 Lloyds TSB (England)

Lloyds TSB is a major banking and insurance group, predominantly UK-based, but with operations in some 30 countries around the world. The corporate vision is to make Lloyds TSB the best financial services company, first in the UK then across borders. In this chapter Lloyds TSB describes how their corporate responsibility strategy is to support the corporate vision by helping to build a great place for people to work, a great place for customers to do business, and generating great returns for shareholders.

3.12 Finally

The experiences recorded in the following chapters are wide-ranging. They cover national quality award models, management models for fair trade, corporate social responsibility, organisational excellence and various aspects of organisational value-chains. It is an intriguing journey into the use of models in different organizational and environmental contexts – a great learning experience for anyone who undertakes it. A great source of knowledge and hands-on insights for those that are in the process of creating their own model.

References

Beauchamp, T.L. and A. Rosenberg (1981). Hume and the Problem of Causation. Oxford University Press. New York.

Eskildsen, J.K. and J. Jonker (2001). Unravelling Relevance – The Nature of Holistic Management Models. in Proceedings (Vol. 2, s. 320-327). Skt. Petersborg: The Stockholm School of Economics in Saint Petersburg.

Guillen, M.F. (1994). The age of Eclecticism: Current Organizational Trends and the Evolution of Management Models, Sloan Management Review, Vol 36, no. 1, p. 75-86.

Hendricks, K.B. and V.R. Singhal (2001). "The Long-Run Stock Price Performance of Firms with Effective TQM Programmes", Management Science Vol. 47 No. 3, pp. 359-368.

Jonker, J. and J.K. Eskildsen (2002, jun.). Intentional Improvement. Paper presented at The 7th World Congress for Total Quality Management

Kristensen, K. and J.K. Eskildsen (2006, jan.). Towards a typology on companies striving for organizational excellence. Paper presented at MAAOE, Sydney, Australia.

Kristensen, K., Juhl, H.J. and J.K. Eskildsen (2003). "Models that Matter", International Journal on Business Performance Management Vol. 5 No. 1, pp. 91-106.

Linder, J. and S. Cantrell (2000). Changing Business Models: Surveying the

Landscape, Accenture Institute for Strategic Change

Ostenwalder, A., Pigneur, Y. and C.L. Tucci (2005). Clarifying Business Models: Origins, Present, and Future of the Concept, Communications of AIS, Volume 15, May

Popper, K.R. (1994). The Myth of the Framework, Routledge, London.

Rüegg-Stürm, J. (2005). The new St. Gallen Management Model: Basic Categories of an approach to Integrated Management. Palgrave Macmillan. New York.

Innovative Models for Steering Organisations: A Systemic Approach Within the Pharmaceutical Industry

The case of CILAG AG

Markus Schwaninger and Matej Janovjak

Abstract. The purpose of this chapter is to draw some lessons from an experience with the creation and implementation of innovative management models. The case in point is Cilag AG, one of the leading Swiss firms in the pharmaceutical industry. The demand for new and better management support has led to an organisational process whose emergence has been brought about with the help of management models at different levels of the business. These range from generic frameworks to detailed simulation models. We are focusing on core components of the Company Management Model. First, the Credo and Standards of Leadership, which provide the normative basis for corporate activities. Second, the Business Model, which includes a business simulation model with front-end cockpits for managers. Third, the Organisational Model, which contains the architecture for an overarching process-oriented design of the organisation. Finally, the Process & Product Model, which delivers maps and instruments as tools for management; quality, compliance and risk management in particular. The models have been created with a high level of participation from people throughout the organisation, under the leadership of the unit of Strategic Process Management & Methods (SPMM), which fulfils the role of an innovative turnplate and catalyst. The results of this approach are so remarkable that the managers are asking for more.

Key words: Model-based management, systemic management model, business model, organisational model, organisation design, management of complexity, System Dynamics

1   Introduction

The pharmaceutical industry is ever evolving and highly competitive. In order to survive, any company must be well aligned with the dynamic context in which it operates. Besides making needed product and process innovations in the company and introducing highly complex new products to the market, the management is challenged to develop new ways of organising and managing.

Cilag AG, located in Switzerland and embedded in the Global Pharmaceutical Supply Group of Johnson & Johnson, has evolved an innovative approach to management to enhance global supply chain excellence. The aim of this paper is to explore that experience in order to extract certain lessons from the case, but also to promote the exchange of ideas.

First of all we need to clarify our understanding of the crucial concepts. Here are our working definitions:

1. A **model** is a (simplified) abstract image or representation of a reality. It can be a replica, a paragon or a standard. Simplification is achieved via definition of the model objectives and focus. As a result, what we call the *model system* is formed in the mind of an observer (mental model) and on paper or in the computer of a modeller (formal model). Close correspondence of the *model system* to the *real system* of interest should be achieved.

2. By **management** we understand the design, (self-) control and development of complex systems, e.g. organisations and processes. We subsume "leadership" under that more general term. Management reverts to the support of management systems which are formal systems made up of components such as models and instruments to enable the design, control and development of a company (e.g., corporate charters, quality management systems, planning and information systems, etc.). The terms *management system* and *management model* are often used as synonyms.

3. **Management models** are models for steering organisations, i.e. models which help those in charge of managing to fulfil their task effectively. Today this group is not limited to managers in the narrow sense of the word. It includes the many persons who have to fulfil some managerial function as part of their overall task, e.g. as project managers, team leaders, staff members, etc.

Management models should support effective leadership and strong performance at all strata of a company. They include broad normative frameworks, which are qualitative, as well as the qualitative and quantitative models at the strategic, tactical and operational levels.

Why are management models so important? The answer is given by the theorem of Conant and Ashby (1981): "Every good regulator of a system must be a model of that system." To paraphrase this, the result of a management process cannot be better than the model on which it is based, except by chance. In other words, the models on which managers operate largely determine what managers can accomplish. Hence, the quality of models is a limiting, but potentially also an enabling, factor for the quality of management.

In the next section we will first introduce the company which is the object of our case study. Then the origins and evolution of the management model will be sketched out. In the ensuing section an overview of the structure and features of the model and two of its crucial components will be given. Then, the experiences with the use of the model will be assessed. The chapter closes with lessons and recommendations for practitioners.

2 Company background

Cilag is one of the major players in the Swiss pharmaceutical industry. It was founded in Schaffhausen, Switzerland in 1936 and became a member of Johnson and Johnson (J&J), the world's most comprehensive and broadly based manufacturer of health care products, in 1959. The firm's activity is deeply anchored in Johnson and Johnson's core system of values, which has characterized the corporation for more than 60 years and is documented in the corporate "Credo". It is focused on the company's responsibilities towards its clients, especially doctors and patients, to employees, communities and stockholders.

"The highest standards of Quality, Health, Safety and Environment friendliness" are pillars of the norms governing the company. Cilag's strategy is orientated toward supply chain leadership in a number of pharmaceutical blockbuster drugs, all of the high-technology type. That implies technological leadership in the new-product-introduction and manufacturing process. This orientation has been dominant since the foundation of the company. While changes in the core business or industry have not occurred, what has changed many times in the course of an evolutionary process is the process technology.

3 The normative framework of the company

The normative framework is essentially condensed in two components, the corporate "Credo" and the "Standards of Leadership". The corporate Credo is the fundamental reference system. It is a condensed expression of the identity and spirit of the organisation. It fulfils a coordinating function bundling all efforts across the company. The corporate Credo is centred on the responsibilities of the company to its stakeholders – first and foremost "to the doctors, nurses and patients, mothers and fathers and all others who use our products and services". The responsibilities also extend to "our employees, the men and women who work with us throughout the world". Here, the Credo adds: "Everyone must be considered as an individual". Furthermore, the responsibilities extend to "the communities in which we live and work and to the world community" (with the imperative "We must be good citizens"), and finally, "to our stockholders" (quotations from Johnson & Johnson, Our Credo).

Based on this Credo, the Standards of Leadership have been established as a second reference system bringing the crucial principles of leadership into focus. They provide a guide to the mastering of complexity. The guide does not elaborate on operational details, but is limited to essentials. It brings into the minds of employees the imperatives of dealing effectively with complexity, innovation, customer and marketplace focus, organisational and people development and interdependent partnering. And it provides advice on how to abide by these principles.

Both the corporate Credo and Standards of Leadership are the most basic models for the orientation and coordination of all employees (at Cilag roughly 1,000, in Johnson & Johnson over 100,000 altogether). In practice, they have a strong impact. They provide a "mental coordination" of the members of the organisation. At a deeper level, they substantially coin the corporate culture, and they enhance cohesion and organisational energy.

As far as the models are concerned, their design is affected by both Credo and Standards of Leadership, as we will show. The basic principles and values propagated therein are reflected in the different models in use; for example, the organisational model refers to different stakeholders. The process and product model has a strong quality and risk orientation. Finally, all models are focussed on coping with complexity.

4   Evolution of the company management model

Over the years, a variety of management systems and models have been developed and used. As far as the conventional management systems for planning and information, accounting, personnel management, etc., are concerned, Cilag has always been well-equipped. These systems were successively improved over the years to a level comparable to the standards of the best-managed companies.

Around the turn of the millennium a "paradigm shift" – to be elaborated on later – occurred. Therefore, we shall focus on a generation of management models which have emerged since the start of this decade, in the wake of both growing complexity on the one hand and progressively increasing requirements from regulatory institutions such as the Food and Drug Administration (FDA), USA. on the other. In such a context, the leadership perspective of managers and also of specialists had to switch from a functional or specialist to a generalist approach which concentrates on the whole reference system rather than on segments or single events. That approach calls for understanding the causal structures and generative mechanisms which induce patterns of behaviour and ultimately produce daily events. It must also be based on a dynamic rather than a static view, and must be not only analytical but also, and even more so, synthetic. Altogether, this new image of management was subsumed under the notion of a *systemic management*.

These new needs triggered a strong movement towards the development of new management systems, models in particular. The quest here was not to improve the accounting system or the information systems, which – measured by the needs – were nearly perfect. Rather, the new demand was for management models which would enable their users to employ a systemic management as envisioned above.

Under the leadership of the unit for Strategic Process Management & Methods (SPMM) the pertinent developments were taken in hand. This unit has understood itself to be a servant of managers which helps them solve their managerial issues and problems, not by intervening or explaining, but rather by knowing managers' "customer problem" and providing them with conceptual and methodological solutions which are "universally valid" in the sense of being widely applicable. The solutions offered by Strategic Process Management & Methods are not advice about what to do or interferences in the discretion of managers. The approach instead is a) to convey new concepts to managers enabling them to evolve their understanding and b) to make available management models which reinforce their managerial abilities on the basis of those concepts. That is, the management models are the vehicles for putting new thinking into practice. That way, in a process of effective learning, managers acquire new abilities while they improve the performance of the organisation.

5 Overview of the company management model

The company management model is embedded in the company's normative framework and embraces several management models on the strategic, tactical and operational levels. Figure 1 gives an overview, without any claim to completeness. On the strategic level are located business, quality and compliance models, on the tactical level the models which reflect organisational and methodological aspects, and on the operational level the models for the technology and manufacturing part of the company.

We shall describe only one characteristic management model for each level. To elaborate on all management models in use would take us beyond the scope of this contribution.

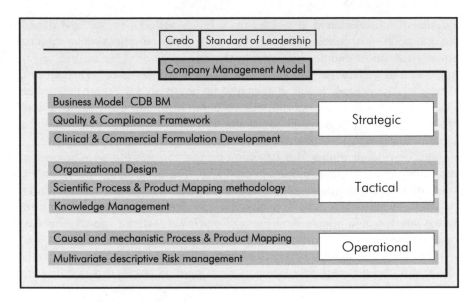

Figure 1. Components of the company management model (extract)

To ensure dynamic devices for management support and to achieve knowledge synergies, all of these models have been developed using the System Dynamics (SD) methodology.

System Dynamics is a widely used methodology for the modelling and simulation of complex systems, which was developed by Professor Jay Forrester at MIT-Massachusetts Institute of Technology. System Dynamics models are made up of closed feedback loops. Feedback is about circular causality: A signal is fed back into itself, i.e., the outcome of a process returns to change the input consequently influencing the process itself.

The systems modelled are simulated as continuous processes, i.e., the mathematics of the models is based on differential equations. System Dynamics is particularly apt for the discernment of a system's dynamic patterns of behaviour, which may be "counterintuitive" (Forrester, 1971). The dynamics are a function of the structure, made up of closed loops as well as delays in the process, and therefore, generally, are non-linear (see also Sterman, 2000).

5.1 The business model

The overarching goal was to create a high-level description which adequately captured the complexity of the business so as to provide managers with a comprehensive decision-support tool.

The Business Model was supposed to be able to simulate the dynamic system behaviour, based on the cause-effect relationships inherent in the business processes and reflected in the company's key performance indicators (KPI's). The model in fact enables managers to deal with complex issues in a pro-active, circumspect and balanced way.

The model was developed in cooperation with external consultants, but the main momentum came from inside the company. Altogether, about 30 experts and Cilag managers were involved in the model development and validation. The purpose of the participative approach was both a) to achieve a buy-in of the representatives of the organisational functions and b) to arrive at a realistic and relevant model. The realism of the model had, in addition, to be warranted by a sophisticated validation procedure by which, among other tests, sensitivi-ties to parameter variations were examined and simulation results were com-pared to real-world data. The modelling and implementation process has been documented elsewhere (Schwaninger, Janovjak, Ambroz, 2006). Here we shall concentrate on describing the model as such.

The Business Model is made up of two components, the Causal Dashboard Business Model (CDB BM) and the Management Cockpit. In the CDB BM the whole company is represented by means of four kinds of variables – drivers, process measures, outcome measures and business results. These are linked by causal relationships, expressed in formulas (Figure 2).

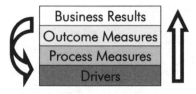

$$DY = F(DY_1, ..., DY_i, ..., DY_n)$$
$$DY_i = F(Dy_1, ..., Dy_i, ..., Dy_n)$$
$$Dy_i = F(DX_1, ..., DX_i, ..., DX_n)$$
$$DX_i = F(Dx_1, ..., Dx_i, ..., Dx_n)$$

Figure 2. The logic of the CDBM BM

The software used was Vensim, a user-friendly and powerful modelling and simulation tool. The Causal Dashboard Business Model is composed of 56 drivers (e.g., leadership, training, knowledge management), 60 process meas-ures (e.g., yield, overtime rate, asset utilization), 50 outcome measures (e.g., cycle time, cost of goods produced, diversity index) and 12 business results (e.g., customer satisfaction index, capital efficiency, profit). These are con-nected by 280 causal relations and 32 main feedback loops resulting in a complex model.

The model's benefit is that it gives its users the opportunity to ask "What-If"-questions, also of the complex type. It may be consulted about what would be the impact of a certain action or set of complementary actions. Conversely, a user can trace what has to be done and how, i.e., which policy variables to use and how to calibrate them in order to reach a certain set of goals. In this way scenarios can be explored and strategy options examined. Ultimately, if this kind of model is applied strategy design can improve substantially and decisions become more robust.

The Management Cockpit is an interface between the Causal Dashboard and its user. It provides a decision environment for managers or whoever wishes to explore the model. It gives users the possibility to view the company's model from any point of view. An example of a screen from the cockpit is shown in Figure 3. The values of external parameters (e.g. factors which impinge on the company) or internal drivers (e.g., investment in training) can be changed and the impact on any variable of the model ascertained. Scenarios can be explored. Features such as sensitivity analysis, parameter optimization, etc., which are standard components of the simulation model, can be leveraged by easy and effective visualization. Sable, the software supporting the cockpit, is easy –to use so that users can customize their decision environment. Extra screens can be added, extant screens adapted, new structural features explored, etc.

The strength of the cockpit must be seen in the context of the Causal Dashboard Business Model. That model is grounded in a feedback perspective which focuses on causal relationships in general and which in particular identifies loops of circular causality (e.g. Production asset capability → Productivity → Profit → Funds → Investment in production assets → Production assets capability → etc.). Consequently, accurate explanations of results, causal tracing of errors, detection of relationships, etc., are enormously facilitated.

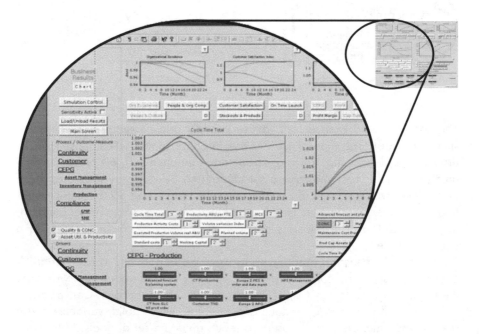

Figure 3. Screen from the cockpit of the Business Model (example)

In other words, the feedback view can indeed make a difference. The model and the cockpit should enable a new way of learning which established management systems have not provided. Playfulness is a feature of utmost importance here. We know that most of the important discoveries of humanity can be traced back to playful exploration. That is exactly what the interaction of humans and computer models is about: a playful approach to the understanding of an utterly complex reality. We expected that understanding would be achieved at a much faster pace than with other known approaches to describing and explaining complex issues. We trusted that, via the interaction of individual or team with the model, decision capabilities would be greatly improved and human intuition might even be sharpened. We knew that experiments with scenarios and even with new model versions are powerful vehicles for learning and developing managerial capability. The point, apart from the strategy of playful experimentation and exploration, is that in the new environment learning would be self-directed.

5.2   The organisational model

In the highly competitive environment of the pharmaceutical industry, companies are facing challenges such as faster expansion into new markets through highly complex new product launches and licenses, in order to obtain the required competitive advantages. Other key challenges are the global alignment of operations as well as the improving and leveraging global product and process knowledge within the steadily increasing complexity of new technologies. Coping with such issues is at the heart of management and leadership in organisations that operate globally.

The key requirement in our case was to create an overarching process-oriented organisational design of globally operated technology platforms within Johnson & Johnson's Global Pharmaceutical Supply Group Europe-Middle East-Africa (GPSG EMEA). The focus here was on key business processes (capacity planning and asset management, manufacturing, new product introduction, etc.). The organisational design has to ensure, among other things, the process-oriented integration of stakeholders into processes and the construction of technology platforms to support and enhance strategic changes in the manufacturing network. As the technology platform serves a group of manufacturing units involving similar technologies and products, knowledge management becomes a key aspect of operation.

The basic structure of the Organisational Design Model consists of four components and their relationships as sketched in Figure 4. The components are:

1. *Processes:* Thirteen key macro processes were identified whose viability is to be maintained, e.g., Technology & Innovation, New Product Introduction, Process Engineering, Asset & Capacity Management, Technology Platform Performance Management.

2. *Stakeholders:* Seven main organisational units were defined as "stakeholders" – Pharmaceutical Technology Services, Marketed Product Services, Business Unit, Human Resources, Quality & Compliance, Technology Platform Engineering, European Logistic Center. The term "stakeholder" refers to the stakes of these units in the success of the firm and their legitimate claims for organisational support.

3. *Knowledge management:* The creation of product and process knowledge, a crucial resource of the firm, has to be boosted through the new Technology Platforms, enhanced through key processes and fostered by focused organisational efforts and measures.

4. *Organisational Excellence:* This is mainly about capability and competence orientation with regard to organisational processes. Process design and leadership are considered as aptitudes with long-term implications, and are at least as important as product-related capabilities. Therefore, they must be cultivated and enhanced systematically.

In order to make the organisational complexity understandable, a cybernetic approach was implemented. Each one of the model's four components is supported

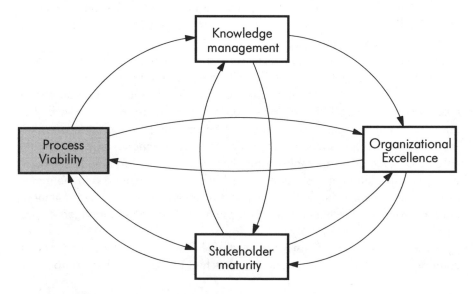

Figure 4. Schematics of the organizational design model

by heuristic schemas and causal maps on the basis of the System Dynamics methodology. These support or capture organisational decisions, e.g., about which processes have to be steered globally, which regionally, what degrees of standardization of the processes are indicated, etc.

Applying the Vensim software, a causal mapping and a simulation model of the relationships between technology platform, related stakeholders and defined key processes were developed. Figure 5 shows the core of the causal map, underlying the simulation model and Figure 6 a graph with simulation results. The different scenarios in the graph indicate the results obtained by working the different handles (expressed in the parameters of the model).

These simulations help actors in the organisation to develop effective and efficient action. The model also facilitates optimisation and provides a well-defined basis for the rollout of global implementation of technology platforms.

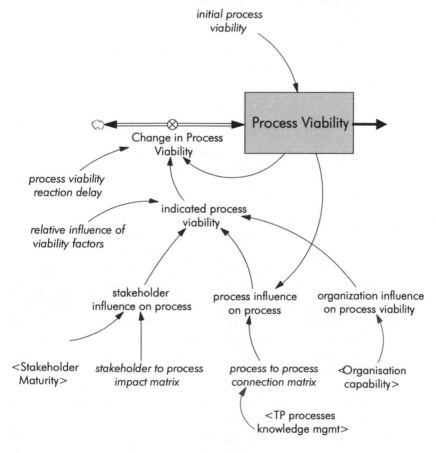

Figure 5. Abstract of the system dynamics model

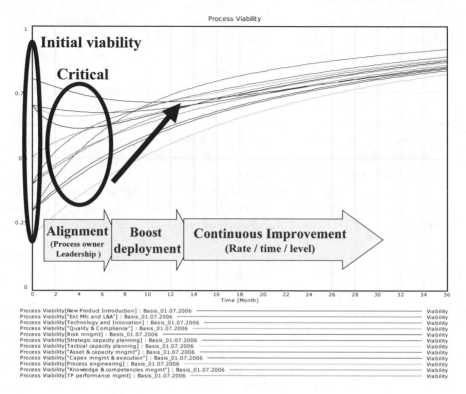

Figure 6. Exemplary simulation results (dynamic behaviour of 'process viability')

5.3   The Process & Product Model

The so-called causal and mechanistic, i.e. quantitative and formalised, Process & Product Maps are the kind of models which have been created at higher levels of resolution than the Business Model. These more detailed maps reach down the cascade from the company level to the level of the individual workplace. An example would be a model of a production unit directed by a group of workers on the shop floor. But these mappings are not only detailed, they also provide an encompassing, holistic picture of the system-in-focus in that they not only show the elements but also the relationships which make it up.

We have chosen to present a model here which is strongly rooted in the production and technology domains. This concentration on manufacturing is of particular interest, because this is precisely where process and product security, reliability, robustness, and compliance with regulations are dominant factors of performance.

The main ideas underlying the Process & Product Model are: Firstly, product and process are two components which are so strongly intertwined that they should be modelled in conjunction. Second is the imperative of an overall view across all the steps of the process of value creation. The third idea is that a causal and mechanistic model on scientific grounds should be provided. Fourth, that the model should be available at a high degree of operational detail. Fifth, the model should be a device which allows a fine-grained steering of the process variables and product quality attributes. Sixth, it should be an effective instrument for anticipating risks. Seventh, the preceding should enable Quality Assurance to better understand and select from the possible process and product variations. Eighth, the model should enable prevention and improve foresight. These aspects are vital in pharmaceutical production where the quest for the health of patients, environment friendliness and compliance are absolute-must criteria. A showcase example of such a product and process mapping is shown in Figure 7.

This is only a conceptual overview of the model. Given the complexity of the process with all its ramifications for chemical or biological analytics, process controls, etc., the overall map would be too large to be reproduced here in a readable way. The diagram shows the conceptual design of the science-based Product & Process Mapping, and indicates links to specific management systems and instruments (e.g., QC-Quality Control, IPC-In-process Quality Control, PAT-Process Analytical Technology).

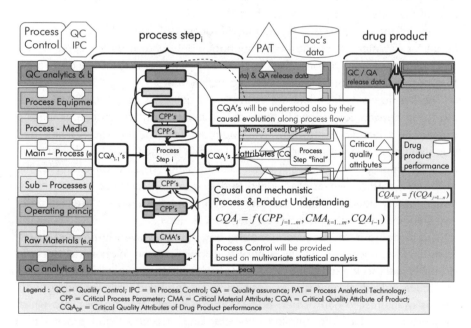

Figure 7. Conceptual design of the Process & Product Model demonstrating mapping structure, causalities, functions and links

This Process & Product Model visualizes, among other things, the cause-and-effect relationships between the critical process parameters, critical raw material parameters and relevant critical quality attributes of the product. Based on this capability, a deep and unambiguous causal and mechanistic understanding of the process and product phenomena is ensured. Hence, the model provides an adequate basis for multivariate risk assessment and continuous improvement. Also, the development and usage of the model enhance an effective and efficient knowledge management that overarches the processes.

As we expected, the kind of science-based Product & Process Mapping shown here, which is the latest component of the management model, is becoming standardized in the company at a fast pace. For example, all stakeholders on the Technology Platform have already deployed this methodology. Potential users can easily see that this new instrument provides them with enhanced analytical and diagnostic strengths. It was clear to us that it makes the detection and elimination of flaws easier and more effective, in comparison with traditional approaches. Furthermore new ways of improving product quality and process performance were within easy reach. Both process and product development as well as technology transfer could be designed with the help of the new mapping technique. Finally, the new approach implies that many can participate in the analysis, diagnosis and design – in principle, anybody who is part of the system modelled in the chart.

In short, at Cilag causal, quantitative Process & Product Mapping has become the key element of knowledge management. As a result the common focus has shifted from a corrective, backward-looking, and re-active orientation to a preventive, forward-looking, and pro-active one.

There is no doubt that different methods of quality assurance today are tending to go beyond corrections in hindsight. The very term "assurance" implies a preventive orientation. However, we maintain that the holistic, causal and quantitative modelling approach with a dynamic feedback view is more potent than the approaches which still dominate the field. To give an example, the fishbone diagrams, which are widely used in quality assurance, are essentially linear representations, which represent neither the dynamic features of processes nor the inter-linkages between the process steps.

The mapping introduced here enables any agent involved in product development, manufacturing, quality control and logistics, from higher managers to group leaders to the individual worker, to gain a higher quality of understanding. Each individual now is in a position to comprehend both the operational details of interest to him or her, and the larger system of reference into which they are embedded. The detailed understanding of product and process also strengthens the company's position towards regulatory institutions (FDA-Food and Drug Administration, etc.). That is a key to superior performance.

6 Experience with the application of the model

The management models established at Cilag offer a new overall perspective. The possibility to experiment at almost no cost, resulting in huge benefits in the form of knowledge and insights, is a great opportunity for managers, and ultimately for decision-makers at all levels. That opportunity, however, is not self-evident. The Strategic Process Management & Methods (SPMM) unit had to fulfil its important role as a deployment driver and catalyst to the understanding and use of the models before the overall picture for opportunity could emerge.

With demonstrations of small models and a dialogue by which model users were closely involved in their design, confidence in these new devices was built up. The interest in these innovations grew quickly. Pioneers adopted them early on. The top managers, as power promoters, soon saw the benefits of modelling and simulation, and some acted as role model users, which were then emulated by a larger number of employees. In the third quarter of 2005, i.e., about six months after the prototype of the Business Model became operational, the management models on the tactical level had been established (Organisation Design, scientific Process & Product Mapping methodology). In the first quarter of 2006, the first scientific Process & Product Mapping came out. No sooner was it presented to the middle and lower level managers in Product Development, Production and Quality Assurance, than the first demands for making the model available for day-by-day use arose. Also, a customisation of the model for their purposes was defined and executed.

The management models were not complete in the early stages and still had to undergo tests for the purpose of validation, i.e. tests to ensure their quality, which in this context refers to accuracy and precision. The question was: "Is the model an adequate reflection of the reality it is supposed to represent?" The types of validity tests embraced not only statistical testing but also qualitative checks.

Essentially, to decide on the validity of the model four types of tests were carried out:

- Behaviour reproduction (i.e., to check if the behaviour of the real systems is appropriately reproduced by the model)

- Structural fit (structure of causal relations, parameter confirmation, dimensional consistency)

- Plausibility and consistency of results (extreme-conditions, sensitivity, qualitative features analyses)

- Validity for application (if the model is appropriate for the domain in which it is to be used and conforms with purpose)

Testing in these four ways gradually built up confidence in the models among the users.

Experience with usage of the models has confirmed our expectations. Beyond that, however, surprising benefits also emerged. The model users, managers in particular, have acquired a new way of looking at events. Increasingly they have switched to a more systemic thinking – that focuses on dynamic wholes, and combines analysis and synthesis. Beyond expectations, they have gradually been learning new ways of managing. Learning takes place at an accelerated pace, because it is learner-centred and self-directed. This new learning proceeds not by instruction but by selection (cf. Olaya, 2007). In the learner's dialogue with the model many variants, e.g., of strategies, can be created; the most promising ones are then chosen and put into practice.

This learning process has not ended yet and probably never will. But a change towards innovative modes of running the business has become evident. Where decisions used to be taken with little analytical underpinning and essentially on the basis of gut-feeling, a new mode of decision-making is taking over. In the first place, people try to understand the system at hand and its workings. Then they go about building a theory – a theory of action which works. They explore the space of action possibilities, test potential measures with respect to vulnerabilities and robustness, and then decide upon a solid foundation.

One significant and promising new feature is that users of the models tend to adhere to a proactive design mode rather than to the traditional, reactive control and intervention mode. Also, an effect of multiplication is visible: The high level of participation has led to a diffusion of the new management style, because many members of the organisation are encouraged to adopt the new practices.

The most striking finding is that a fundamental transformation to a new logic of management has been taking place. This surprising transition has even been considered a "paradigm shift" – not only by the Head of the Strategic Process Management & Methods unit (author M.J.), but also by several line managers involved. It shifts paradigms because the management and staff are adopting a new, shared view on how to manage their company.

7   Insights and recommendations

An overall outlook on what has been achieved with the models discussed here calls attention to several results which are discernible in hindsight, but which reach beyond what had originally been expected. The original idea was to provide a set of models which would help the agents in the company to cope with the complexities they faced in more effective ways. However, as it has now turned out, the management practice at Cilag has undergone a "paradigmatic change". Managers and staff have learnt a new way of making decisions and of discovering new approaches to running their business.

Even though one must concede that not each and every manager in the company subscribes to the new "paradigm", one can see a generation of managers emerging for whom the work with the models is a natural feature of their daily practice.

What are the teachings of this case? The following points are not scientific principles. They are, however, a set of pragmatic recommendations which can help in finding paths toward more useful management models:

1. **The quality of the model determines the quality of management.** This calls for powerful models, in other words models which give an accurate picture of the reality faced by those who use it. Such a model must open new spaces and enhance the repertory of behaviour (also called the "potential variety") of managers and staff. It must be integrative, dynamic, and sufficiently rich.

   Don't work with too simple or weakly founded models. Illegitimate simplification and trivialization tend to lead to erroneous conclusions which may lead to disastrous consequences. At the same time, excessive complexity of models must be avoided as well, because their workings will prove to be untraceable and it will become more difficult to distinguish between what is important and what is not.

2. **Design a holistic company management model.** A company should have an overall framework which – like a genetic code – defines the identity and the spiritual architecture of the organisation, in particular its fundamental principles and values. It is essential to design the whole management system in a coherent fashion. The management models on the strategic and tactical levels should be holistic in that they integrate different dimensions, e.g. social, economic, technological and ecological. They should also help individuals orientate themselves in relation to the whole, i.e., the larger system in which they operate.

   While embracing a holistic view, avoid a scattered approach: Fragmented and one-dimensional models proliferate short-sightedness and undermine the necessary co-operativeness which crosses borders.

3. **Conceive management models for dealing with the crucial issues.** In our case company the number one challenge is growing complexity. The management models are fully concentrated on that issue. For example, the Business Model as well as the Causal Process and Product Model enhance the capability of actors for dealing with complexity more effectively: their behavioural repertoire is amplified by them.

   Don't try to model everything. Your model will lose both rigor and relevance. In other words, it will be neither good (valid, reliable) nor practical.

4. **Incorporate a dynamic view and make it operational.** In a complex environment, integrative and dynamic models are called for. These should be equipped with extensive simulation capabilities, and an interface that enables careful analysis. Such facilities should foster the learning and improvement of the dynamic view, the thinking in causal relationship and operational thinking of users. The thinking in feedback loops should become a routine. The feedback view makes a difference in that it helps to progress from mere analysis toward synthesis and understanding.

   Don't get caught in the reductionist logic of open causal chains. These do not take into account the retroaction of the system you are dealing with. Avoid the trap of the misleading static models. Be careful to avoid the seductiveness of excessive abstraction, which is alienated from the functioning of the real world.

5. **Make modelling and simulation a widely used practice.** Let people discover the crucial relevance of good models, in both minds and computers. Support self-directed learning. Foster conceptual thinking through learning-by-doing, courses and modelling workshops. Dedicate enough effort to the understanding of the complexities in which the organisation and its individuals are immersed. Let theory-building for a better practice become a widely adopted routine.

   If the people in your company do not like to use models, don't accept that attitude. Make sure that managers discover the importance of models in order to improve their decisions.

6. **Make management models focus on the long term.** Orientate yourself vis-à-vis the long term, and give the long-range perspective priority over the short-term viewpoint. This is not to forget about the here-and-now, but to be clear about the relative weights of the different imperatives. A long-term orientation can be difficult and costly in the short run but, if it succeeds, the dividends are high. This reflection is valid for all key business aspects (company development, outreaching compliance, new technologies, etc.).

   Avoid the error of founding your strategic scenarios or plans on extrapolations from historical data only. Design your models in a way that lets them incorporate adaptations and new inputs.

7. **Design and implant the management models in a participative way.** Involve the future users of the management models in their design and deployment. Help as many people as possible to leverage the models for conceptualizing and understanding their business better. This way they should arrive at a more circumspect way of making decisions, thinking about and exploring options, and examining consequences of actions as well as the opening of new spaces for action. Last but not least, participa-

tion should enhance the results and robustness of the company. Ultimately it should catalyze the viability and development of the organisation.

Do not succumb to the specialist syndrome. In this constellation a few experts elaborate models which then are made available to "the rest". This way of proceeding is counterproductive – a source of weak models, and of non-acceptance, misunderstanding and indifference or conflict.

8   The challenges ahead

Trends in the pharmaceutical industry from 2007 – 2009 are characterized by the increased impact of generic pharmaceutical competitors, decreased R & D productivity, cost pressure and sustained high performance (in terms of growth and gross profit) of biopharmaceutical products.

From the perspective of management and organisation the following issues are among the challenges which might play a key role:

- The need to master more complex technologies and supply chains
- High requirements on leaders' capabilities in environments with increased complexity and accelerated changes
- Increased needs for superior organisational capabilities (e.g., development of core competencies and knowledge, innovation, process orientation).
- Compression of development time for commercial product design, to reduce time-to-market.
- Diverse changes of business environment (e.g., pressure on profits, extensive collaborations, merger integration).

Management models will help in coping with these issues, and they will have to be developed further as well.

References

Conant, R.C. and W.R. Ashby (1981). Every Good Regulator of a System Must Be a Model of that System. In: Conant, R. (Ed.). *Mechanisms of Intelligence. Ashby's Writings on Cybernetics.* Seaside, California: Intersystems Publications, 205-214.

Forrester, J.W. (1971). Counterintuitive Behavior of Social Systems. *Technology Review*, 73, No. 3, 52-68.

Olaya, C. (2007). *Evolutionary Governance.* PhD dissertation. University of St. Gallen, Switzerland (forthcoming).

Schwaninger, M., Janovjak, M. and K. Ambroz (2006). Second-Order Intervention: Enhancing Organizational Competence and Performance. *Systems Research and Behavioral Science*, 23, 529-545.

Sterman, J.D. (2000). *Business Dynamics. Systems Thinking and Modeling for a Complex World*. Boston, Massachusetts: Irwin/McGraw-Hill.

Websites

For Cilag's Mission, Corporate Credo and Standards of Leadership:
http://www.cilag.ch/

For Information about Johnson & Johnson: http://www.jnj.com

For Johnson & Johnson Europe and Middle East: http://www.jjeurope-csr.com

An Integrative Model of Corporate Volunteering

The case of Henkel

Christa Büchler, Christine C. Schneider, Jan-Dirk Seiler-Hausmann, and Kai von Bargen

Abstract. Henkel's social commitment is firmly embedded in its corporate values and its corporate history. Launched in 2005, the Henkel Smile program brings together all aspects of Henkel's social commitment – internationally known as corporate citizenship – that go beyond its business activities. Henkel Smile unites four modules, one of which is the MIT (Make an Impact on Tomorrow) Initiative, which support the volunteer work of Henkel employees and pensioners. The MIT Initiative focuses in particular on the involvement of employees and pensioners who identify social challenges, develop innovative solutions to these challenges and make them known within the Company. As corporate volunteers, they are active ambassadors of the company at all Henkel sites throughout the world.

Key words: Corporate citizenship, social commitment, Henkel Smile, corporate volunteering, Corporate Social Responsibility (CSR)

1   Introduction

Sustainability means future viability. We are convinced that sustainable development must give equal priority to economic, ecological and social goals. Only economically successful companies will be able to contribute to effective environmental protection and social progress. Developing and producing innovative products that make people's lives easier, better and more beautiful are a core element of Henkel's sustainability principles.

As a company that operates worldwide, Henkel is called upon to play its part in advancing sustainable development. In our Values, we have declared our dedication to sustainability and corporate social responsibility (CSR), and we assume this responsibility wherever Henkel operates. For us, sustainability and corporate social responsibility are synonymous. We contribute to society through our brands and technologies that make people's lives easier, better and more beautiful, while always striving to harmonize economic, ecological and social objectives. In short: Henkel – A Brand like a Friend.

The challenges we face are global, but priorities and perspectives vary considerably from region to region. We accept these global challenges and work to solve them locally, in more than 125 countries around the globe. Throughout our 130-year history, we have drawn inspiration and motivation for all that we do from people's trust – their trust in Henkel.

People in the different countries and markets in which we do business have different values, customs, expectations and needs. These differences are taken into consideration by our employees all around the world.

All aspects of Henkel's social commitment that go beyond its business interests – corporate citizenship – are grouped under the "Henkel Smile" program. Our employees and pensioners know best what the local challenges and needs are. Their volunteer work is therefore a valuable element of our CSR strategy. Within the framework of the Make an Impact on Tomorrow (MIT) Initiative, they support their project ideas throughout the world with enthusiasm, understanding, helpfulness and personal commitment. Our employees are an important bridge between Henkel and society: Viable solutions for the future can only be developed through a dialogue with the social groups in each of the communities in which we operate. Henkel views the dialogue with its stakeholders as a challenge and a source of new ideas and wants to share its experience with others. The dialogue with social groups helps Henkel to assess local and regional challenges and define key areas for its activities.

2 Company background

Henkel is headquartered in Düsseldorf, Germany. It operates in three business areas: Home Care; Personal Care; and Adhesives, Sealants and Surface Treatment. Today, Henkel is the world number 3 in the laundry and home care market, among the global top ten in cosmetics and toiletries, world market leader in consumer and craftsmen adhesives, and also world market leader in the field of industrial and structural adhesives, sealants and surface treatment technologies.

People in 125 countries around the world trust in brands and technologies from Henkel. In 2006, Henkel generated sales of EUR 12,740 billion. Henkel employs 52,292 people worldwide – 80 percent of them outside Germany.

Henkel's long-term strategy is to concentrate on its three business areas and further expand its leading market positions globally. A regionally balanced portfolio is a key element of this strategy. Since 2005, Henkel's top sales region has been North America. It is considerably more profitable than the Western European market and has excellent growth potential. Besides North America, the Asian market will be a further focal point. Henkel wants to achieve a larger share of its sales there than at present. It also aims to expand further in the growth regions of Eastern Europe, Africa, the Middle East, Asia-Pacific and Latin America.

"Quality from Henkel" is a group-wide maxim. This promise of quality is linked to core corporate values such as customer orientation, innovation, human resources development, sustainable development and corporate social responsibility. In order to secure and expand its leading market positions, Henkel is putting its faith in the innovation capabilities of its employees. 2006 will remain in the corporate memory of Henkel as its "Year of Innovation". The response has already been impressive, with 71,000 new ideas submitted to a central database by the end of February 2007. The campaign will be continued through 2007 and 2008. Innovative thinking, speed of reaction and the utmost flexibility are required not only at work but also in volunteer projects. The Henkel Smile projects are shining examples of the connection between motivated employees, social commitment and corporate success.

3   History of the corporate social responsibility management model

Sustainability and corporate social responsibility have been a permanent feature of Henkel's corporate history since its earliest beginnings. Already company founder Fritz Henkel based his decisions on economic, ecological and social considerations. In 1880, for instance, reacting to protests from local residents and problems with a building permit, he had his first water glass factory in Düsseldorf built with a higher smokestack than originally planned. Fritz Henkel also provided company housing, meals and medical assistance which went beyond the employees' work environment and into the family sphere (see Timeline, 130 years of Henkel, published 2006).

Henkel's sustainability strategy is embedded in its Vision and Values and is also an integral part of its management systems. The starting point for today's management systems was the company's objective of ensuring the ecological safety of its products and production. Today, worldwide management systems for safety, health, environment (SHE Standards) and quality are in place at Henkel, and the concept of sustainability and corporate social responsibility is firmly anchored in its corporate policy.

Henkel is firmly convinced that sustainability stands for future viability. Henkel aligns its business practices to the principles of sustainability because it believes that this is the key to achieving sales and profits in a socially responsible manner. This philosophy applies to all of the company's activities – throughout the value chain.

Table 1. Milestones of sustainability orientation

1876	Fritz Henkel founded Henkel & Cie in Aachen; workforce: 3 employees; manufacture of the first product named "Universal Laundry Detergent" based on water glass.
1878	First successful brands for home laundering in Germany: Henkel's "Bleich-Soda" (bleaching soda), a powdered mix of soda and water glass.
1878	Relocation of the company from Aachen to Düsseldorf-Flingern. Fritz Henkel arranges for office workers to receive free copies of the Düsseldorfer Stadtanzeiger (a local newspaper) to keep them up to date with current affairs.
1900	Free midday meal for employees every day, construction of the first company apartments for employees.
1907	Persil was developed as the first self-acting laundry detergent. It relieved housewives of the laborious rubbing by hand and the attendant wear and tear on the fabric.
1911	Sport and games areas were provided for use during breaks.
1912	A first-aid centre was set up at the plant and a full-time nurse was hired.
1917	Henkel employees elected their first representative body (workers' council).
1927	Henkel became the first company in the chemical industry in Germany to employ a safety engineer who was responsible for planned accident prevention. Alongside his safety tasks, he sought to improve work conditions.
1933	A welfare station was established on the site to offer advice to mothers, as well as care for infants and medical examinations for children.
1934	Since 1927, systematic accident prevention work had reduced the number of accidents per 100 employees per year from 10 to 4.
1940	Organization of a plant kindergarten as well as a site medical service staffed by volunteers.
1959	Introduction of regular ecological quality checks for detergents and household cleaners.
1969	Launch of the solvent-free Pritt glue stick and Persil 70. The enzyme-containing Persil 70 was given the claim "biologically active."
1971	Setting up of the central department for environmental and consumer protection.
1976	Launch of Proxidan – the first branded laundry detergent with reduced phosphate content.
1976	Management Principles (since 1996: Guidelines for Teamwork and Leadership)

Table 1 (continued)

1980	The first in-vitro tests were carried out in place of animal testing, energy saving campaign as a consequence of the second oil crisis.
1982	The first Fritz Henkel Awards for Innovation were presented to employees.
1986	Principles of Environmental and Consumer Protection (since 1995: Principles and Objectives of Environmental Protection and Safety)
1986	Launch of phosphate-free Persil in Germany.
1987	Environmental protection is included as one of the aims in Henkel's corporate guidelines.
1990	Systematic environmental protection training courses for all employees of Henkel KgaA.
1991	Establishment of a works agreement on „Family and Work" between Henkel KGaA and the Works Council.
1991	Signing of the Business Charter for Sustainable Development of the International Chamber of Commerce (ICC).
1992	Publication of the first Environment Report.
1994	Corporate mission: Competitive advantages through eco leadership.
1995	Publication of Guidelines for Teamwork and Leadership, which are binding for all Henkel employees worldwide.
1997	Introduction of integrated management systems, binding company-wide SHE standards for safety, health and environment, and launch of worldwide SHE audits.
1998	Founding of the MIT Initiative.
2000	Introduction of Code of Conduct and Business Ethics.
2001	First Sustainability Report.
2001	To mark the 125th anniversary of Henkel, support provided for 125 country projects.
2003	Declaration of participation in the United Nations' Global Compact.
2004	Grouping of worldwide social responsibility activities under the umbrella of Henkel Smile.
2005	Introduction of Code of Corporate Responsibility.
2006	SHE Standards supplemented by social standards and purchasing guidelines throughout the company.

To further the group's systematic alignment to sustainability, Henkel relies on group-wide targets and requirements, efficient management systems, and an organisation structure with clearly defined responsibilities. The interplay of globally uniform standards, group-wide control instruments, and regional action programs is key to these efforts. Achievements and advances can thus be identified and – where improvements are possible and necessary – programs can be optimally aligned to the respective social challenges and priorities. The Henkel Management Board bears overall responsibility for sustainability policy and aligns the company's business policy to the requirements of sustainability and corporate social responsibility.

The Henkel Management Board bears overall responsibility for sustainability policy and aligns the Company's business policy to the opportunities for and requirements of sustainable development. The Sustainability Council, whose members are drawn from all areas of the Company, steers the global activities in collaboration with the operative business sectors, the regional and national companies, and the corporate functions. ⓘ

Figure 1. Sustainability organisation

In all business areas and cultures in which Henkel operates, its Vision and the ten Values derived from it provide guidance for the behaviour and actions of all Henkel employees. Henkel's Vision and Values form the basis for a series of behavioural rules for Henkel managers and staff, which are specified in a number of codes, e.g. the Code of Conduct, the Code of Teamwork and Leadership, and the Code of Corporate Sustainability. The Code of Corporate Sustainability defines the principles and expectations of sustainable business practices and corporate social responsibility at Henkel. The Code expresses Henkel's view of its responsibility in concrete terms. It covers nine aspects: economic success through sustainability, individual responsibility and motivation, safe and environmentally compatible products and technologies, safe and efficient plants and production processes, treatment of business partners and market

Figure 2. Vision and values

behaviour, sustainable business processes, technology and knowledge transfer, management systems for clear responsibilities and continuous improvement.

Together, the Codes are the basis for Henkel's implementation of the United Nations' Global Compact initiative. Companies joining the Global Compact accept the challenge of positioning themselves to help achieve the United Nations Millennium Development Goals and playing an active role in developing practical approaches toward doing so.

The Code of Corporate Sustainability is given concrete form by internal standards. The standards are based on the existing requirements for safety, health and environmental protection, which have been comprehensively revised and given a new, process-related, structure. They are supplemented by requirements for social responsibility and by group-wide purchasing guidelines. Henkel is committed to supporting and promoting sustainable development in the 125 countries in which the company operates. The basis for achieving this is Henkel brands and technologies which are designed to make a valuable contribution to society.

3.1 Henkel Smile – Henkel's commitment to corporate citizenship

In 1998, Henkel launched its MIT Initiative, a concept which, in the intervening years, has proved to be a successful model for involving the company's employees and pensioners in corporate volunteering. Based on the success of the MIT Initiative, Henkel formulated a corporate citizenship concept, consisting of four modules, to bring together the widely varied activities that Henkel already pursued in this field. Since 2005, the four corporate citizenship modules have been grouped under the umbrella of "Henkel Smile."

3.2 Corporate volunteering – the MIT initiative

The strategic involvement of employees and pensioners in our corporate citizenship approach has steadily grown in importance over the years. One milestone was the founding of the MIT Initiative, which takes the volunteer work of employees and pensioners as a starting point for creative and efficient project support. The implementation of this innovative corporate volunteering concept started with a business trip to the USA. In 1997, impressed by what he had seen in the USA, a member of the Management Board asked a team of employees to examine whether corporate volunteering could be introduced at Henkel.

On January 1, 1998, the MIT Initiative was launched. This special form of corporate volunteering, which supports existing projects in which our employees and pensioners do volunteer work, puts the emphasis on teamwork. In the very first year the expectations were far exceeded: Henkel employees and pensioners submitted around 60 applications requesting support for the organisations and initiatives in which they were involved on an honorary basis. Today, nine years after the founding of the MIT Initiative, there have been more than 1,125 MIT-supported children's projects and more than 4,574 MIT-backed community projects, all benefiting either financially or through in-kind and product donations. Today the MIT Initiative is the best-known instrument of the Henkel Smile program.

4   Description of the current management model

For Henkel, corporate social responsibility is a wide-ranging concept. "It is no longer simply about ecological advances, or promoting cultural projects or supporting a social idea," the Chairman of the Management Board, Prof. Dr. Ulrich Lehner emphasizes. "It is primarily about how a company behaves in its pursuit of profit. The important thing is that a company demonstrates social responsibility in all its activities, throughout the value chain." Henkel faces a wide variety of social challenges and local priorities in the various regions and market segments in which it does business. On the basis of worldwide standards, Henkel therefore seeks to give due consideration to the values, needs and expectations of people in different countries and markets, so that it can contribute to sustainable development.

All aspects of Henkel's social commitment that go beyond its business interests – corporate citizenship – are grouped under the "Henkel Smile" program. With the Henkel Smile program, we want to convert our vision to be "A Brand like a Friend" into fact. Henkel takes its role as a member of society seriously and assumes the associated responsibilities actively and with full commitment. We want to help solve societal problems through a flexible and targeted approach, and in a spirit of partnership.

What is this commitment based on? The long-term objective of Henkel Smile is to strengthen the positive reputation of the company and, in countries where there is a low level of awareness of Henkel, to make the company better known. Involving employees and pensioners in this program increases motivation at the workplace, loyalty, and identification with the company. Committed employees expand their social competencies and stimulate team building in the workplace. Potential highly qualified employees are attracted to the company. The focus on the sites results in the formation of stable cooperations and alliances, which simplifies the dialogue between the company and its stakeholders. Furthermore: "A company that accepts its social responsibility can integrate itself more easily in a variety of cultural settings and is more open to the changing demands of multicultural markets," says Prof. Dr. Ulrich Lehner. "It is able to resolve any conflicts more easily, fulfil the expectations of the different stakeholders more efficiently, and is therefore simply more successful."

The employees and pensioners are an important element in the Henkel Smile program. They supply project ideas, draw attention to cases where help is urgently needed, and make an active contribution to solving social problems. They are the company's ambassadors. They inject life into the guiding principle and the core promise "A Brand like a Friend" and translate them into action.

By supporting the involvement of our employees and pensioners, we ensure that our assistance is channelled to where it is needed most. Similarly, we involve our brands and technologies and also our business partners and sponsorship partners actively in such undertakings, constantly launching new initiatives and collaborations in the process.

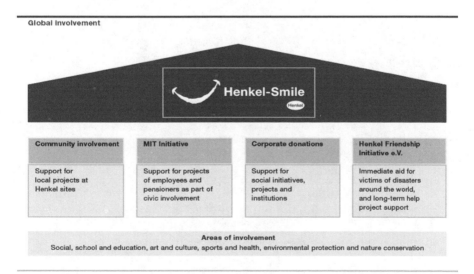

Figure 3. Global areas of corporate involvement

Henkel supports projects under the headings Social Welfare, Schools and Education, Art and Culture, Sports and Health, and Environment.

The four modules are employed flexibly, on the basis of the initial situation of the project. The significant role of our employees and pensioners can be seen most clearly in the MIT Initiative. The employee or pensioner and the Company act as a team in which each partner makes his own contribution. An employee who does volunteer work in his free time is provided with support by Henkel in the form of financial, product, or in-kind donations. The employees themselves ensure that all resources are used transparently. If a project is especially time-intensive, limited paid time off from work may be accorded.

This enables employees and pensioners all over the world to help alleviate local problems while, as the project heads, they play a pivotal role as a link between the company and its social environment. They are in a position, in each individual case, to assess the socio-cultural settings and local differences and to take personal responsibility for the transparent use of funds in nearly 105 countries.

Since its inception in 1998, the MIT Initiative has sponsored 4,574 employee projects, contributing more than EUR 9 million– not including the cost of paid

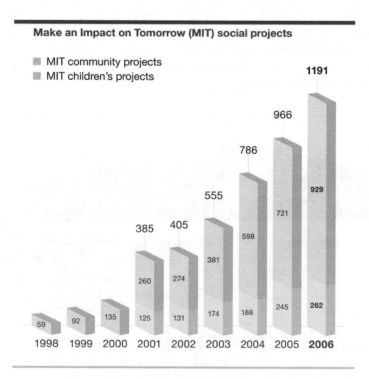

Make an Impact on Tomorrow (MIT) social projects

- MIT community projects
- MIT children's projects

Figure 4. Social project under MIT program

Table 2. Selected Henkel Smile projects

Social The social challenges at the locations of the Henkel sites differ widely throughout the world. The spectrum ranges from a shortage of nursery schools to inadequate care for senior citizens and problems of racial discrimination.	**USA: New home for survivors of Sudanese civil war** In Arizona, Henkel Smile supports the "Lost Boys" centre, which offers a home and prospects for a new future to young refugees who have escaped the chaos of the civil war in Sudan.
Education and science Knowledge is one of a society's most valuable resources. To promote the conditions for an independent life, with equal rights, for as many people as possible, Henkel supports in particular the provision of training and continuing education at schools, as well as equal access to knowledge and educational opportunities for all.	**Germany: Awards of grants and scholarships** Henkel awards grants at various educational levels to help young people in their studies. The Hugo Henkel Award supports schools that focus mainly on teaching science. The Jost Henkel Foundation awards scholarships to talented students in the fields of economic, social, natural and engineering science, while other awards are available to university graduates who have performed outstandingly in natural and economic science disciplines.
Culture and leisure Cultural and artistic leisure activities are a source of pleasure and creativity. Group leisure activities also promote social competence. Henkel therefore focuses on supporting creativity in the form of artistic development.	**Brazil: Classical music lessons for disadvantaged children** In a project of the religious Assembléia de Deus Nipo Brasiliera, which takes care of children from poor families, Henkel Smile supports employees who give the children lessons in classical music and help them to become familiar with a variety of instruments.
Sports and health Sports and health are closely related. Regular exercise counts as one of the most important activities for staying healthy. Worldwide, not everyone can afford medical care. Henkel therefore supports projects aimed at providing comprehensive medical care. Projects that promote health by encouraging sports activities are also supported.	**Nepal: Medical aid for more than 1000 refugees** For the seventh time, Henkel employees organised the transport of aid donations to a Tibetan refugee camp in Katmandu. A team of doctors and medical students provided medical care and supplied the refugees with medications and hygiene articles.
Environment Henkel has a long tradition of supporting environmental protection and environmental education. In many regions, Henkel takes responsibility for projects aimed at preserving conservation areas or threatened animal species.	**Ghana: Support for sustainable agriculture** Henkel employees and the Agricultural Rural Association (ARA) are building an agricultural training centre in which ecological methods of farming, e.g. using reforestation, will be taught.

days off from work. The projects are divided into two categories: MIT Community Projects are selected independently by each individual site and supported by funds from the national donation budget. The support in this category is not limited to a specific age group. The range of project types aided this way is therefore very broad indeed, extending from care for the elderly and assistance for schools to local anti-racism projects and support for volunteer fire brigades. The decision-making process: National MIT committees meet four to five times a year. Maximum grant: EUR 5,000 per project. The MIT Children's Projects have been selected centrally for all Henkel companies once a year since 2001 and allotted EUR 1 million of support annually. Of the 1,125 MIT Children's Projects sponsored up to now, 262 projects were carried out in 2006 alone – a figure that demonstrates the dynamic growth of the MIT Initiative. The decision-making process: The international Children's Projects Jury convenes once a year in order to go through the new applications and decide on the funding levels appropriate in each case. Maximum funding: EUR 10,000 per project.

Selected Henkel Smile projects as they relate to the United Nations' eight Millennium Development Goals

Millennium Development Goals	Henkel Smile projects (2006)
1. Eradicate extreme poverty and hunger	**Moldavia:** Financial support for an orphanage in Falesti **Cameroon:** Improving medical care in Fongo Ndeng **India:** Building a children's village for orphans and children from broken families in Tirunelveli **Dominican Republic:** Building a new orphanage (Casa Santa Anna) in Babey Nuevo **Argentina:** Providing food and health aid for families below the poverty line in Buenos Aires
2. Achieve universal primary education	**Nepal:** New classrooms and a library for the Samudayik Vidya Mandir school in Mandir **Bangladesh:** Literacy campaign for children in the district of Mollahat **Laos:** Building a new school, complete with furniture and sanitary facilities, in Muang Phong **Tanzania:** Private school for teaching small groups to a high standard in Karagwe **Romania:** Help with homework for children from socially deprived families in Caransebes
3. Promote gender equality and empower women	**Tanzania:** Education and vocational training for girls in Rogorv **Uganda:** Furnishing a dormitory for a girls' boarding school in Kabale **USA:** Girl Scout project in San Francisco, California, to promote self-reliance **USA:** Project to help young girls in Detroit, Michigan, to plan their careers
4. Reduce child mortality	**Ukraine:** Equipping a hospital in Kiev with life-saving equipment for newborn babies with brain tumors **Kenya:** Provision of medications for children with lymph node cancer in Mkomani **Germany:** Acquisition of a microplate reader for the University Children's Hospital in Düsseldorf to help research children's infectious diseases **Turkey:** Acquisition of respirators for newborn babies in Gaziantep
5. Improve maternal health	**Peru:** Medical support for underage mothers and their children in Ventanilla, Lima **South Africa:** Help for mothers with disabled children in Pretoria **Togo:** Support for a mother and child center and AIDS station in Lomé
6. Combat HIV/AIDS, malaria and other diseases	**Thailand:** Medical care for HIV-infected orphans in Lopburi **Rwanda:** Reconstruction of a home for AIDS and war orphans in Kigali **Tanzania:** Construction of a school for AIDS orphans in Leguruki **Malawi:** Providing care for AIDS orphans and arranging for them to stay with relatives in Lilangwe
7. Ensure environmental sustainability	**Niger:** Construction of a well to supply drinking and irrigation water in Fouangbe/Sekrere **Tanzania:** Construction of a new well for a vocational training school in Mashi **Hungary:** Educational activities centering around environmental protection in Körösladány Nature Park
8. Develop a global partnership for development	**Ghana:** Summer camp for the renovation of a school in Agona Swedru and reforestation in Biakba **Brazil:** Acquisition of equipment and machines for the vocational training of young people in Passo Fundo **South Korea:** Support for a soccer team for children of Mongolian workers in Seoul **Spain:** International youth soccer tournament to promote cultural exchanges in Malgrat

Figure 5. Henkel project related to millennium goals

4.1   Henkel Smile and the contribution to global development goals

Through the non-profit projects of Henkel Smile, Henkel and its employees help to improve the quality of life of many people by alleviating their situation or simply making them happy. This commitment goes beyond these individual benefits, however, and achieves much more; it contributes toward addressing worldwide problems and challenges. In the year 2000, in its Millennium Development Goals, the United Nations identified the urgent social and political issues of the present and the future and formulated eight goals to be reached by 2015. Through Henkel Smile, Henkel makes many small contributions towards the achievement of these goals – especially in developing and emerging countries.

5   Deployment of and experiences with the management model

Henkel has been supporting its employees' commitment to charitable projects since 1998. Initially, this was driven by the corporate headquarters and the German employees. The further development of the corporate citizenship activities was then concentrated under the Henkel Smile program. Today nearly all countries where Henkel operates are involved through their employees. Through the MIT Initiative, Henkel makes many small but important contributions that go beyond its business interests, helping to achieve its philanthropic goals especially in developing countries and emerging economies, where more than half of the MIT projects are carried out.

The Henkel Smile program and in particular the MIT Initiative are key elements of Henkel's human resources policy. Henkel's employees contribute to the success of the company – also in areas beyond its business activities. One of Henkel's ten values is "We are successful because of our people." Corporate Citizenship is therefore no abstract challenge, but is a commitment shared by all employees and pensioners. Employee involvement in the form of corporate volunteering is integrated in the five pillars of Henkel's human resources policy:

1. Motivated employees are the basis for Henkel's success.

2. At Henkel, sustainability is not the task of a group of managers, but it is the task of all employees.

3. Respect for individual diversity and principle of equal treatment is anchored in our Code of Conduct.

4. Worldwide employee share program.

5. Programs to maintain and improve employee health.

The MIT Initiative has snowballed. Today, employees and pensioners are involved not only in their own projects, in self-established MIT networks and in

Table 3. Milestones of the MIT initiative

1998	Launch of MIT community projects in Germany
2001	Launch of MIT children's projects worldwide
2002	Roll out of MIT community projects worldwide
2007	Central corporate budget for international MIT community projects

the MIT database, they also serve as local contacts for colleagues at their own and other sites.

Any successful development inevitably has to overcome barriers, and this was also the case with the global rollout of the Henkel Smile program. A prerequisite for the involvement of employees and pensioners in a given cultural environment is that volunteer work and the acceptance of civic responsibility are widespread and accepted there. This is not always self-evident in some of the regions where Henkel sites are located, for example in Asia or in the Arab world. Due consideration therefore has to be given to the cultural background. Striking a balance between local circumstances and expectations on the one hand and centrally defined corporate activities and involvement profiles on the other is a continuous challenge. Volunteer work has a different significance in different cultural environments and must therefore be adapted to the local circumstances. Broad acceptance has been achieved within the company by defining uniform standards (for example with regard to the project-support criteria), by nominating contacts, and through intensive internal communication.

The globally adjusted implementation of the Henkel Smile program has already won several awards in Germany and abroad:

Table 4. Awards

2006	Koerber-Foundation, Germany, honours the MIT Initiative in the Transatlantic Idea Contest "USable"; topic: Transitions in life.
2005	Government of North Rhine-Westphalia, Ministry of Economic Affairs and Labour, honours the Henkel Smile program with the "ENTERPreis"
2004	UNESCO honours the MIT children's project „Baan Gerda"
2003	Agenda 21 – Best Practice Example, awarded by the Government of North Rhine-Westphalia
2003	Children's Charity of Germany honours the MIT children's projects with the "Goldene Goere" award
2003	The national contest "Freedom and Responsibility" honours the MIT Initiative with second prize

6 Some dos and don'ts

Dos	Don'ts
1. Global standards but maximum possible flexibility at the individual company sites (e.g. standardized forms, selection processes, project controlling). This is especially important for the implementation at sites that have different cultural settings (e.g. different volunteer cultures).	1. Use of employees and pensioners as instruments to achieve corporate ends. As instrumentalisation can be a very sensitive issue it might be helpful to involve the employees and pensioners right from the beginning in terms of concept development, project selection criteria etc.
2. Clear selection criteria for project sponsorships	2. Mixing corporate citizenship activities with classic marketing (although there is a grey zone, e.g. issue-related marketing)
3. Balance between central steering (headquarters) and local/decentral adaptation at the sites. Possible instruments on central and/or decentral level: round tables, project jury, communication tools and strategies, databases etc.	3. One-sided focus on employees without involving pensioners
4. Organic growth: Corporate citizenship instruments should be in harmony with corporate culture and history, and develop organically in the company	4. Top-down strategy, with no due allowance for local circumstances, culture and mentality
5. Clearly defined instruments (quality takes precedence over quantity). Possibility of flexible application, e.g. for long-term cooperation projects or immediate aid after natural disasters	5. Failure to communicate corporate citizenship activities, e.g. out of a feeling that one should "do good deeds but not talk about it" or: One-sided communication (either too factual or too emotional)
6. Flexible communication strategies: a) Balance between factual information and emotional reports about "everyday heroes" b) Good balance between internal and external public relations	6. Too much focus on external communication (internal communication is at least as important!)
7. Continuous networking with all reliable partners in society (local, regional, national, international)	7. Failure to embed CSR activities in a strategic overall concept

7   The future challenges and how the model will be adapted to meet these

Henkel still faces challenges with regard to the global rollout of Henkel Smile:

1. The global Henkel Smile standards will be expanded even further in the future. This will cover the project-support criteria, the decision-making processes and associated committees, and communication strategies. A manual will help with the implementation of Henkel Smile at sites throughout the world. The www.henkel.com/smile website will also be completely revamped to facilitate the continued global rollout of the model.

2. Employees and pensioners will be encouraged to participate in the Henkel Smile program to an even greater extent. The intention is to involve employees and pensioners at all levels more strongly in concept development, corporate volunteering and in providing local support, for example through local employee networks. An annual "round table" already brings together employees and pensioners who are involved in the MIT Initiative and gives the Management Board an opportunity to express its appreciation. There are plans to organise round tables decentrally in the future and to upgrade their significance through a combination of internal exchange of information and external project presentation. In addition, internal communication of the Henkel Smile program will be continuously expanded, e.g. through the intranet, the employee newspaper "Henkel Life" and an annual Henkel Smile pocket calendar, which will be distributed to all employees and pensioners.

3. The local adaptation of the Henkel Smile program will be given added emphasis in the future. This will require due sensitivity to be shown with regard to local social problems and priorities, especially in developing and emerging countries.

4. The visibility of the Henkel Smile activities will be enhanced by an appropriate communication strategy. Internally, the business case in particular will be clearly highlighted.

5. Dialogue with the stakeholders is of crucial importance with regard to the company's commitment to align its business practices with the requirements of sustainability and corporate social responsibility. The company is cooperating with internationally renowned experts with the aim of ensuring that its corporate social responsibility addresses current global and local issues. This dialogue with experts will also be conducted with regard to corporate citizenship. Only in this way can Henkel measure up to its claim to be a "good citizen."

References

Henkel (2007). Henkel Sustainability Report 2006

Henkel (2005). Code of Corporate Sustainability

Henkel (2005). Code of Conduct

Henkel (2005). Henkel Smile 2004/2005

Henkel (2006). Henkel Smile 2006/2007

Henkel (2006). Timeline 130 years of Henkel

Websites

http://www.henkel.com

http://www.henkel.com/sustainability

http://www.henkel.com/smile

Managing the Value Chain in a Large Nordic Bank

The case of Danske Bank

Kai Kristensen, Lars S. Mørch, and Henrik D. Sørensen

Abstract. The scope of the study is to analyze the relationship between employee satisfaction and motivation on one side and customer loyalty and customer profitability on the other in Danske Bank. Danske Bank is the leading financial institution in Denmark and one of the largest and highest rated in the Nordic region. Danske Bank has for many years measured and analyzed various aspects of business performance. In 2002 Danske Bank and Ennova, the partner of Danske Bank in performance measurement, teamed up with Center for Corporate Performance at The Aarhus School of business in order to set up a scientific approach to the analysis of performance measurement data. This lead to a project, from which some of the results are presented here. The main conclusion is that in Danske Bank there is a very significant relation between satisfied and motivated employees and the bottom line results of the bank. This relationship holds good whether you are focusing on sales or whether you are focusing on costs.

Key words: Customer satisfaction, employee satisfaction, link to bottom line, value chain

1 The companies: A short presentation of Danske Bank, Ennova and the Centre for Corporate Performance

Danske Bank is a leading financial group in northern Europe. The Group, whose head office is in Denmark, conducts a wide range of financial services focusing on retail banking. Before the recent acquisition of Sampo Bank in Finland (late 2006) the Group's asset base amounted to DKr 2,400bn (320bn EUR) and the Group employed more than 19,000 persons.

Danske Bank is the largest bank in Denmark and a leading player in the Scandinavian financial markets. The Danske Bank Group – which includes Danske Bank, BG Bank, Realkredit Danmark, Danica Pension and a number of subsidiaries – offers a wide range of financial services, including insurance, mortgage finance, asset management, brokerage, real estate and leasing services.

In 2004 Danske Bank stepped out of the Nordic region and announced the acquisition of Northern Bank in Northern Ireland and National Irish Bank. The acquisition marked the end of a phase dominated by share buy backs and modest growth, and the start of a distinct growth phase.

In Denmark, Norway, Sweden, Northern Ireland and the Republic of Ireland, the Group serves 3.5 million retail customers and a significant part of the corporate, public and institutional sectors. It also has a large number of international corporate clients, particularly in the northern European markets. Some 850,000 customers use the Bank's online services.

In the period 2003-2005 the total return on the share has been 94 percent including price appreciations, dividend and share buybacks. US investors hold approximately 13 percent of the shares, which is the largest proportion outside Denmark.

Ennova is a leading Nordic consultancy specializing in performance measurement and management. The main focus of the company is advanced analytical modeling of key intangible assets with the ambition to deliver actionable business diagnostics to managers and hereby strengthen business performance.

Offering services under the business areas Customers, Employees, Reputation as well as Integrated Reporting, Ennova has in recent years established a position for itself as the leading player in the market for Performance Measurement and Management in Denmark.

On the basis of advanced analyses, sophisticated IT tools and commercial insight, Ennova produces informative, intuitively comprehensible and action-oriented analyses and consultancy that help customers to strengthen their performance through targeted improvement initiatives.

Today, Ennova's customer portfolio includes the biggest players in the financial sector, industry and manufacture, building and construction, the supply industry, the retail sector, IT, media, education, health and public service and administration. To these can be added a large number of small and medium-sized businesses.

50% of Ennova's revenue stems from international projects. A number of our projects are conducted globally for Danish and international customers. Ennova has more than 60 permanent employees, of whom 80% have a master's degree or higher degree.

For the last five years Ennova has been among the fastest growing Danish companies. The clients include a number of the most successful Nordic companies including Danske Bank.

Center for Corporate Performance at the Aarhus School of Business is a research organization devoted to the analysis of business performance from a scientific point of view. CCP is partly financed by corporate sponsors including Danske Bank.

2 The history behind performance measurement in Danske Bank

Danske Bank has for a number of years focused the effort of HR on structured performance data aligned with the Group HR strategy. As a part of a yearly HR cycle in each of the Groups' brands, e.g. Danske Bank and BG Bank, data on HR is compiled into an HR key figure analysis to be discussed with the head of brand. Based on the conclusions of the discussion a HR action plan is developed and implemented for the coming year.

A part of the structured work on HR performance management is the documentation of HR as a business case. Thus advanced statistical analysis has been done on the correlation of e.g. employee satisfaction and earnings per employee with significant results.

3 Mapping the value chain

Danske Bank has in cooperation with Ennova measured customer satisfaction/loyalty and employee satisfaction/motivation on a detailed basis since 2002. Ever since the start the basic assumption has been that the two concepts are important and significant contributions to the value chain of the bank. Hence it was decided, when data was of a sufficient size, to perform an empirical test of the proposed value chain from employee motivation over customer loyalty to financial results.

In this section we describe the available data, which are coming from different sources, both internal and external, and from different years. Furthermore we describe the proposed value chain, which of course focuses on employee satisfaction/motivation and customer satisfaction/loyalty, but which also includes efficiency elements like employee absence.

3.1 Data

The basic dataset is the corporate employee satisfaction survey with approx. 15.000 responses annually in 2002, 2003 and 2004. This dataset has been combined with the annual customer satisfaction survey in order to identify the relationship between employee satisfaction and motivation on one side and customer satisfaction and customer loyalty on the other. The models behind the two surveys are both of the structural equation type and they include both manifest and latent variables. In both cases the latent variables have been estimated using the well-known partial least squares algorithm. Detailed information on the characteristics (demographics) of both employees and customers has been added to the dataset. It goes without saying that data has been organized in such a way that all demands concerning anonymity was respected.

Financial performance measures from 2002, 2003 and 2004 including sales performance and budget fulfillment has been added to the dataset. This will make it possible to identify not only the relationship between customer loyalty and financial results but also to trace the relationship back to employee satisfaction and motivation. Furthermore data on absence and other internal productivity measures has been included.

Basically the unit of analysis is either the employee or the customer. However, in certain cases especially in the analysis of sales (top line) and the analysis of absence, is has been necessary to aggregate the data to branch level. In this case branch demographics was added to the dataset.

3.2 The value chain in operation

The purpose of the research project was to study the relationship between employee satisfaction & motivation, customer satisfaction, customer loyalty and a number of internal financial performance measures. The data are analyzed on three levels: Individual employee level, individual customer level and on branch level.

The model was estimated using a number of different statistical/econometric techniques. Among these we may mention standard regression and analysis of

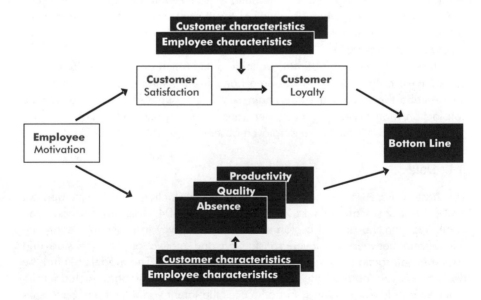

Figure 1. The value chain

variance techniques. For employee satisfaction and customer satisfaction structural equation modeling based on partial least squares (PLS) was used (see Kristensen and Eskildsen (2005)). The theoretical framework behind employee satisfaction and customer satisfaction were the EEI model (see e.g. Eskildsen, Kristensen & Westlund (2004)) and the EPSI Rating model (see e.g. Kristensen, Martensen & Grønholdt (2000)) respectively.

It will be seen that the value chain consists of two perspectives: The top line perspective (sales) and the efficiency perspective (productivity). The top line perspective assumes that given employee and customer characteristics an increase in employee motivation will lead to an increase in customer satisfaction, which again leads to improved customer loyalty followed by increasing financial results. The efficiency perspective assumes that improved employee motivation will lead to improved productivity expressed through among other things improved quality, improved processes and reduced (voluntary) absence.

4   Analyzing the value chain: Top line perspective

The relationship between employee motivation and customer loyalty

Employee satisfaction & motivation and customer loyalty are strongly related on an individual employee and customer level. Dividing employees into three equally large groups leads to the conclusion that average customer loyalty is 3-4% higher for customers served by the most satisfied & motivated employees. The three groups are shown in figure 2.

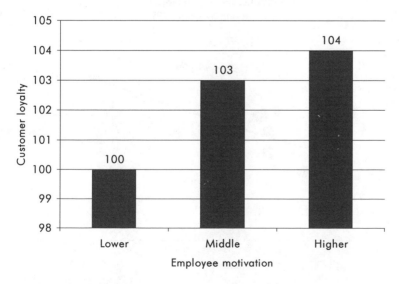

Figure 2. Employee motivation and customer loyalty

Although the difference is clearly significant, the difference may not seem very large. So, in order to put this into perspective we will have a closer look at the theoretical relationship between financial results and customer loyalty. It may be shown that theoretically the elasticity of customer value with respect to loyalty is equal to

$$e = \frac{l}{1+i-l}$$

where l is loyalty (retention rate) and i is the internal rate of interest. Thus if loyalty is e.g. 75%, the elasticity will be close to 3 (see e.g. Kristensen (2004)). The result is based on the assumption that the contribution from existing customers is constant and equal to C. In this case the present value of the customer base will be:

$$CV = \frac{C}{(1+i)} + \frac{Cl}{(1+i)^2} + \frac{Cl^2}{(1+i)^3} + ... = \frac{C}{(1+i-l)}$$

Computing the first order derivative of CV with respect to l and converting into elasticity will directly lead to the result above. The result can easily be modified if the assumptions are changed (e.g. to include a growth rate of C).

This theoretical result is supported by studies of the Nordic banking sector which indicate that the elasticity of ROA with respect to loyalty is the area of 2-3.

**ROA (Consolidated) and loyalty
Denmark and Sweden 1999**

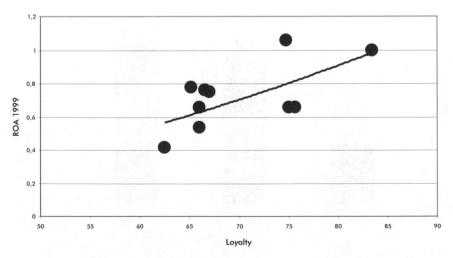

Figure 3. Return on assets and perceived loyalty for the Nordic banking sector 1999

Figure 3 shows a reproduction of a figure from Kristensen and Westlund (2004). It shows results from the Nordic banking sector in 1999. The average elasticity of the curve is very close to 2 and the average loyalty is very close to 70. If we use the formula above and assume that the rate of interest is 5%, we arrive at an elasticity of ROA with respect to perceived loyalty exactly equal to 2! Thus it seems that theory is in very good accordance with practice in this case.

4.1 The relationship between employee motivation and customer profitability

To estimate the influence of employee motivation on customer profitability, the following model was set up:

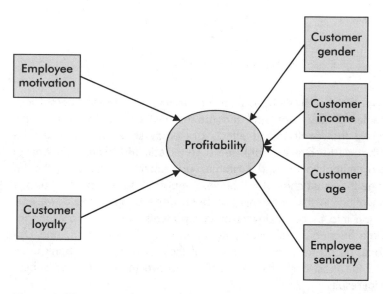

Figure 4. The estimated model of customer profitability

When estimating this model using standard regression techniques, we find that all the factors of the model are statistically significant. Especially employee motivation and customer profitability are strongly related on the individual customer level. One of the partial results is shown in figure 5.

Figure 5 demonstrates that when we are splitting the employee satisfaction and motivation into three groups in the same way as was done in figure 1, we find that customer profitability for customers served by the high motivation group is almost 40% higher than for the lower 1/3 group of employees. This is a very significant result and it seems that the relationship is even stronger than we expected from the theoretical results.

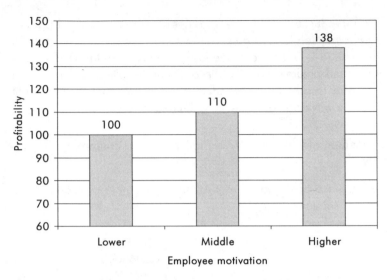

Figure 5. Employee motivation and customer profitability

As appears from the model we have been controlling for several external factors like customer gender, age and income as well as employee seniority. Hence we believe that confounding effects are pretty small in this case. The conclusion is that we for Danske Bank see a very clear and strong relationship between employee motivation and customer profitability. This means that in order to manage the value chain it will be very important to be able to manage employee motivation. In the bank this has been done by breaking down employee motivation into its basic drivers or components: Image, Top Management, Immediate Superior, Daily work, Remuneration, Cooperation, and Development. Focusing on the most important of these it has for the bank been possible to find the most cost efficient way to improve motivation and subsequently financial results.

4.2 The relationship between employee motivation and sales at branch level

Employee satisfaction & motivation and the ability to achieve sales targets we found to be strongly related at branch level. This was demonstrated using a regression model, where we at branch level related data from 2002 to data from 2003. Our endogenous variable was the change in sales budget fulfillment from 2002 to 2003. As exogenous variables we chose: Change in employee motivation, change in manager's motivation, average employee age, manager's age and the gender composition of the branch. An exploratory analysis had shown that these variables were particularly good indicators of sales budget fulfillment.

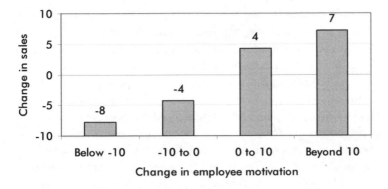

Figure 6. Top line results for branches

Our statistical analysis showed that an improvement in employee and manager satisfaction & motivation leads to an almost 1:1 improvement in budget fulfillment. As a simple demonstration of this we have plotted the change in employee satisfaction against the change in budget fulfillment in figure 6. The results are very significant, both from a statistical and a performance management perspective.

We find similar results for the change in the manager's satisfaction. The higher the change in motivation, the higher the change in sales. A simultaneous change in average employee motivation and manager motivation will be an important way to improve sales in the branches.

4.3 The relationship between the variability of employee motivation and top line results

It has for some time been the assumption among economists that the variability in a unit of various performance indicators may affect among other things the

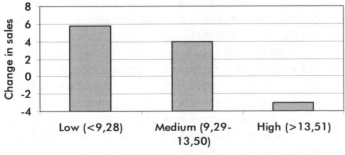

Figure 7. Variability of perceived cooperation and top line results

productivity of the unit. In order to test this hypothesis we had a closer study of one of the components of employee satisfaction, viz. cooperation. For each branch we computed the standard deviation of the perceived cooperation and related this to the change in sales budget. The result of this is seen in figure 7.

The analysis shows that profitability in a branch is strongly dependent on the variability of several aspects of employee satisfaction. The higher the variability the lower the performance. It appears from figure 7, where branches have been grouped into three groups according to their variability in perceived cooperation that those branches, which have a relatively low standard deviation of the performance measure are doing considerably better than those branches, which have a relatively high standard deviation. For the top one third of the branches with respect to variability there has even been a drop in sales performance.

This observation seems to be a rather general one and it seems to be in good accordance with the general assumption within quality management that quality costs are an increasing function of the variability.

5   Analyzing the value chain: Process perspective

5.1   The relationship between employee satisfaction and motivation and internal productivity

The last part of this research project has been dealing with the effect of employee motivation on absenteeism, which was defined as the number of absence periods for a given employee. This was the first of a number of planned projects, which deal with the lower part of figure 1: The effect of employee motivation on various aspects of internal productivity.

The absence study has already been documented in Kristensen, Juhl et al. (2006), and it shows that employee absenteeism is strongly related to employee satisfaction & motivation and especially the cooperation and compensation parts of employee satisfaction. Other factors that showed a significant relationship with absenteeism included the manager's absence, the gender and age of the employee and the location of the branch.

The effect of location was particularly strong and it showed that branches located in highly urbanized areas had a significantly higher absence rate than other branches. This observation is not one which is unique to Danske Bank. Subsequently interviews with a number of other Danish companies have revealed that this is a rather general phenomenon. A phenomenon which probably will have many explanatory factors behind it among which we will find both cultural and social factors.

Among other factors leading to increased absence we find the manager's. If the manager's absence is increasing the average absence of the branch is likely

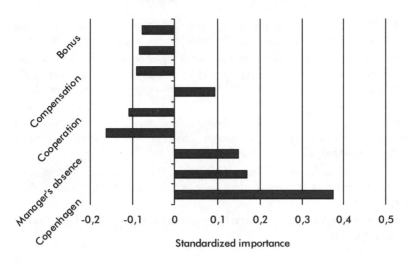

Figure 8. Importance of different factors for controlling absence

to increase as well. Furthermore it seems that the age of the manager plays a role. The older the manager the higher the average absence of the branch.

Among factors leading to decreased absence we find satisfaction with compensation and bonus. Furthermore satisfaction with the cooperation in the branch is important. In general we find that a considerable number of factors from the employee satisfaction study are closely related to absence. Hence the information included in this study provides valuable data for controlling this part of the value chain.

6   Future perspectives

These very interesting results on both individual and branch level have made it clear to Danske Bank that there is a strong relationship between employee motivation and the financial results of Danske Bank. Hence the use and analysis of performance measures will be intensified in the future.

A planed research project will concentrate on employee turnover and employee satisfaction. Furthermore a study of satisfaction segments is being planed in order to be able to identify improvement efforts on the individual employee level.

References

Eskildsen, J.K., Kristensen, K. and A. Westlund (2004). Work motivation and job satisfaction in the Nordic Countries, *Employee Relations*, 26, 122-136.

Kristensen, K. (2004). Image and satisfaction surveys – EPSI Rating and the Danish Customer Satisfaction Index (in Danish), *Scandinavian Insurance Quarterly*, 85, 41-48.

Kristensen, K. and J.K. Eskildsen (2005). PLS structural equation modeling for customer satisfaction measurement: Some empirical and theoretical results. In Bliemel, F.W., Eggert, G. et. al. (eds.): *Handbuch PLS-Pfadmodellierung – Methode, Anwendung, Praxisbeispiele*, Schäffer-Poeschel, Berlin.

Kristensen K., Juhl, H.J., Eskildsen J.K., Nielsen J., Frederiksen, N. and C. Bisgaard (2006) Determinants of absenteeism in a large Danish bank. *International Journal of Human Resource Management*, 17, 1645-1658

Kristensen, K., Martensen, A. and L. Grønholdt (2000). Measuring Customer Satisfaction: a key dimension of business performance, *Int. J. Business Performance Management*, 2, 157-170.

Kristensen, K. and A. Westlund (2004). Performance Measurement and Business Results, *Total Quality Management*, 15, 719-733.

Fostering Co-ownership in Sustainable International Value Chains

The case of AgroFair

René Leegte, Jeroen Kroezen, and Dave Boselie

Abstract. In the past two decades the international food retail sector has been dominated by two major trends: a) increasing consumer concerns about the sustainability of production and trading practices from a human, ecologic and economic point of view, and b) a process of enlargement of scale in production and trade and a rapid spread of supermarkets around the globe. As the supermarket sector develops, leading chains are rapidly adopting technological, organisational, and institutional changes in their product procurement systems. These changes alter the market that farmers face, and have the potential to substantially transform the nature, composition, and volume of trade. These trends in turn present both opportunities and challenges for development, especially of less advanced and small producer organisations in the third world. There has been growing evidence that small producer organisations risk being excluded from the markets.

AgroFair applies a business model that provides an answer to gaining market access for smallholder producers. One of AgroFair's central pillars is the concept of co-ownership in a vertically integrated supply chain. The credentials are embedded in its vision statement : *A Fair Price, A Fair Say and a Fair Share.* Fifty percent of the shares of the company are in the hands of the international producer cooperative CPAF (Cooperative Producers AgroFair) while the other fifty percent is in the hands of European NGOs and sustainable venture capitalists. Based on its business model it has reached the status of preferred supplier to leading retailer COOP Swiss which has enabled it to capture 40% of the Swiss banana market with its fair trade certified products. Recently Finnish SIWA made a similar choice due to AgroFair being a company that explicitly proliferates the co-ownership of Latin American and African producers and the development impact on communities of smallholder producers and workers. Since 2004, AgroFair's turnover has been growing with double digit figures; in 2006 it reached EUR 66 million with a net profit of more than EUR1 million. This chapter describes the history of the AgroFair business model and analyzes the crucial elements that contributed to its success.

Key words: Fair trade, corporate social responsibility, co-ownership, value chains, fruit exports

1   Introduction: Challenging the conventional fruit system

Bananas are grown almost exclusively in developing low-income countries. Most of the bananas are actually consumed in the producing countries. The total of the world's production averaged 92 million metric tonnes in the period from 1998 to 2000, yet only 11.7 million of these were exported to consumer countries in the North (Arias et al., 2003). As bananas are edible only up to six weeks after being picked, the banana industry is strongly vertically integrated. This means strong control (often ownership) over plantations, packing plants and shipping.

For a very long time the global banana export industry has been highly concentrated, with just three companies (Dole, Del Monte and Chiquita), accounting for 55-60% of world trade, and two other companies, Fyffes (in the EU) and Noboa (in the USA), controlling another 25% (Arias et al., 2003). The "big Five" sell their products directly to large supermarkets or to independent ripeners (bananas are picked and shipped green and ripened to order in ripening facilities using ethylene gas).

This high concentration has led to more and more intensive production methods and an intensive price battle. The banana sector has been an important pillar of the Latin American economy since the 1950s when rising prices and an increasing demand in industrialised countries led to a rapid expansion of production. Increased production has been achieved both by improving yields and increasing the areas under cultivation. However, at the beginning of the 1980s, it had become virtually impossible to improve yields significantly in Latin America. As a result, in the past decades or so the increase in exports from these regions has been achieved mainly through increasing the amount of inputs (fertilisers and pesticides) and the area under cultivation. This had huge negative human impact for producers, workers and host countries. The vast plantations are also the cause of negative environmental impact including soil erosion, water pollution, deforestation and a steady increase in pests and diseases that can only be fought by means of more harmful pesticides.

Furthermore it has become clear that smallholder producer organisations face serious threats of being excluded from international value chains (Reardon 2006, Van der Meer, 2006). The increasing concentration in the retail industry demands economies of scale, while increasing quality requirements demand substantial investments in converting production systems and complying with quality standards. Smallholders have difficulties in meeting these requirements.

However, since 1996 the introduction of the fair trade standard in the fresh fruit sector has proven a successful initiative giving smallholder producers access to the rapidly expanding supermarket segment in many European countries. Besides favourable conditions for production and trade, the fair trade movement mobilized substantial technical and financial support for small producers to build up their capacity. One of the core principles of the fair trade standard, the minimum price guarantee, enabled producer organisations to comply with the requirements of sound agricultural practice and to respect social criteria like minimum wages and workers' right of self-organisation.

The focus of AgroFair has been on increasing fair trade fruit volumes. AgroFair shareholders realise that volume creates impact for producers. Increasing the volumes of bananas (or other fruits) sold directly relates to more farmers or workers benefiting and becoming able to improve their circumstances. El Guabo, an Ecuadorian cooperative and one of the first fair trade fruit cooperatives in the world, set out in 1996 with 20 farmers. Now, ten years later, more than 300 farmers produce bananas according to fair trade criteria. Additionally, more then 2000 workers and families benefit from this method of production.

By focusing on volume growth, AgroFair became the world's market leader in fair trade fruits. Other companies introduced sustainable concepts and a number of them fair trade fruits. All these developments pushed the market as reflected in the graphic below (figure 1).

The fair trade impact has not been limited to the third world. AgroFair's constant focus on market development pushed the fair trade fruit market in the EU. AgroFair's entry into the European banana market has transformed the global

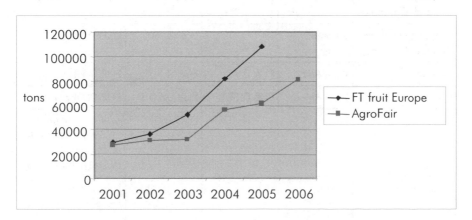

Figure 1. Historical development of volumes of fair trade fruit

banana industry (Alex Nicholas and Charlotte Opal (2004)). Dole and Del Monte are currently pursuing Social Accountability International certification for their company-owned farms in response to growing pressure from consumers and retailers. All Chiquita's company-owned farms carry the Rainforest Alliance label.

While welcoming the progress towards sustainability by the mainstream industry (embracing new social and environmental standards), it is important to realize that the fair trade standard sets the highest criteria and goals for achieving socio-economic wellbeing for producers and workers by incorporating important ILO regulations, minimum cost price guarantees and by enforcing democratic principles in producer organisations. As such it includes pro-poor elements that are an integral part of the fair trade principles laid down in the standards of the Fair Trade Labelling Organisation (FLO) in Bonn. FLO e.v. is an independent organisation developing the standards and FLO cert. (a separate organisation from FLO e.v.) certifies local producers if they are compliant to the standard.

There are basically two different standards: one refers to the smallholder organisations and basically guarantee a minimum price for products based on a cost price calculation (Free on Board: FOB). The other standard refers to organisations with hired labour. This standard will guarantee minimum wages for

Table 1. Fair trade premiums as set by FLO standard

Fruit	Country	FT farm-gate price per kg	FT minimum FOB price per kg	FT premium
Pineapple (MD2)	Ghana		USD 0.60	USD 0.05 per kg
Pineapple (Smooth Cayenne)	Ghana		USD 0.45	USD 0.05 per kg
Organic pineapple (Smooth Cayenne)	Ghana		USD 0.60	USD 0.04 per kg
Mango	West Africa	EUR 0.70	EUR 0.80	EUR 0.14 per kg
Organic mango	West Africa	EUR 0.80	EUR 0.90	EUR 0.14 per kg
Banana	Ghana		USD 8.00	EUR 1 Premium on top of the fair trade minimum price USD/18.14 kg box
Organic banana	Ghana		USD 10.00	EUR 1 Premium on top of the fair trade minimum price USD/18.14 kg box

employees with access to worker unions, social security insurance and other working conditions (toilets, maximum working hours, etc, etc.).

For both standards (smallholder and hired labour) a fair trade premium is transferred to the Joint Bodies which are a representation of smallholders or workers. The Joint Bodies deposit these premiums in a separate bank account. These premiums go toward community activities according to plans approved by the Joint Bodies. The Joint Bodies' plans for the deployment of the premiums and the social activities implemented form part of the FLO audit. This should guarantee that premiums are used according FLO regulations stating that the communities must be the beneficiaries according the approved plans of the Joint Body.

Table 1 illustrates the fair trade premium paid per kilo of fruit in Ghana and other fruit exporting countries in West Africa.

2   The origin of AgroFair

The story of Agrofair is a story about values. In the early 80s the Dutch NGO Solidaridad established "Max Havelaar" as a Fair trade Certification label. In the mid-90s it developed a label for bananas, within the fair trade system. The label was based on both social and environmental criteria. This was the first time that environmental criteria were incorporated into fair trade criteria because to a large extent the social problems in banana production were intertwined with poor environmental practises. As none of the established banana companies at that time were interested in introducing fair trade bananas, Solidaridad set up AgroFair. AgroFair became a 100-% fair trade company, co-owned by its producers.

The fair trade banana model developed by AgroFair, and later adopted by FLO (the Fair trade labelling organisation in Bonn), applies to both cooperatives of small family farmers and to plantations that employ farm workers (Alex Nicholls and Charlotte Opal 2004). Both models use two familiar fair trade components: a fair trade minimum price designed to cover costs of sustainable production (including ensuring liveable wages and decent working conditions for farm workers) and a social premium to be spent on continuous social and environmental improvements. Workers MUST be organized as opposite of an often used phrase as the freedom to organize.

AgroFair's achievements are impressive. AgroFair became profitable in 1999 and now sells fair trade fruit in 13 EU countries, Switzerland and the USA. AgroFair now has a full fruit basket of mangos, pineapples, citrus fruit and bananas. Offices have been set up in Finland, Italy, France, UK and the USA (see figure 2).

Initially AgroFair met with many difficulties. The European Union had a complex system of country import quotas for bananas, designed to protect banana

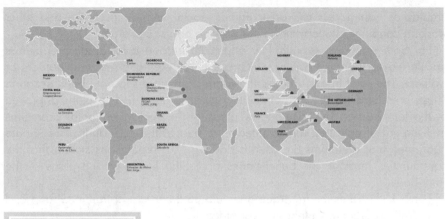

Figure 2. Overview of AgroFair supplier groups and offices

farmers in the EU and in former Dutch, French and British colonies in Africa and the Caribbean. In the early 90s the European Union took two strong measures to intervene in the banana market. This was a compromise between member states when the Single European Market was formed in 1994. These were prompted by a political wish to protect domestic EU production (Canaries, Guadeloupe, Martinique) and weak economies in former European colonies. They introduced a Tariff-Quota system; the distribution of import quota became managed with licences that were divided amongst European importers. The quota system determined the maximum volume of bananas imported into the European market to 15% under the historic consumption level (EU production is domestic), as a consequence of which prices increased by 30%. Because of the ensuing shortage a system was established based on licences allowing the holder to import bananas. The distribution of licenses was based on historical imports. For newcomers in the banana market a negligible potential quota of 3% was reserved.

AgroFair's fair trade initiative was heavily frustrated by the European importing system. As AgroFair had no historic import reference, it hardly got any licenses. The only way to enter the market was to buy licenses and build partnerships with other licence holders, which AgroFair managed to do.

The core activity of AgroFair and Solidaridad has been EU lobbying to change the highly discriminating import regulation. AgroFair argued for preferential market access for sustainable production, rather then preferential access on a geographical basis determined by colonial history. This, however, was not considered compatible with WTO regulations. Since January 2006, the quota system has been suspended. And has been replaced by a tariff-only system in which banana importers from ACP countries are benefiting from a zero tariff. The ACP States are the countries that are signatories of the Lomé Convention. "ACP" stands for "Africa, Caribbean, and Pacific." The Lomé Convention is an ambitious cooperation programme between 27 countries of the European Union and 71 countries in Africa, the Caribbean and the Pacific (ACP). It is based mainly on a system of tariff preferences which give those countries access to the European market and special funds which maintain price stability in agricultural products and mining products

Despite all AgroFair's adversities and the resistance by the establishment to allow a new entrant into the European banana and fruit market, AgroFair has gradually penetrated the supermarket segment which used to be dominated by the Big Five. AgroFair combined a number of unique elements to support this market penetration. AgroFair's products have been fair trade certified and sold under their own recognizable Oké brand. This means that they are certified by FLO, the independent certification and auditing organisation which is an independent body that monitors compliance with fair trade rules and regulations. FLO is based in Germany and was set up in 1997 as an umbrella organisation to coordinate the work of the national fair trade initiatives and run the monitoring programmes more efficiently. These national initiatives, like Max Havelaar in the Netherlands, give companies that want to import fair trade products a license and they have an important role in increasing consumer and customer awareness of fair trade. They do not import any products themselves.

Furthermore, in contrast with the traditional banana companies AgroFair has a different focus on vertical integration. AgroFair's approach can be called "bottom up supply chain integration": the third world producer is integrating the supply chain in his own interest. The producer not only grows the product, but also organises logistics, at the same time having a voice and vote in the sales strategy. Involving producers in business structures, making them co-responsible for the marketing strategy is a viable aspiration (Roozen and van der Hoff, 2003)

So, the idea to establish a organisation like AgroFair was based on an innovative business model. Cooperatives of banana producers became shareholders of the company. This not only guaranteed them of a fair price for their products but enabled them to truly participate in the strategic discussion of AgroFair's mission and vision. AgroFair producers discuss the sourcing and the market development strategy of their own company. This is enriching for the organisation. Above all, as shareholders they receive a share of the profit in the form of dividend.

Alongside an innovative business model stands an innovative market strategy. AgroFair introduced its Oké brand into a sector where traditionally brands barely exist. The Oké brand enabled AgroFair to communicate directly with

consumers and "pull" their fruit products through the supply chain into the supermarkets.

AgroFair's existence is the result of Solidaridad's vision and a partnership between Solidaridad, Max Havelaar, Ambtman – an independent Barendrecht-
based ripener –pioneer farmers from Ecuador and Ghana and a number of
retailers who believed in the fair trade concept. AgroFair's strong focus on innovation also led to the introduction of fair trade pineapples, fair trade citrus,
and fair trade mangoes. AgroFair was the first to introduce these products.

3   The AgroFair business model: A fair price, a fair say and a fair share

The AgroFair business model aims at linking producer organisations in twelve
countries in Latin America and Africa directly to supermarket customers in various European countries. AgroFair Europe has its headquarters in Barendrecht
in The Netherlands, and operates as an importer, distributor and marketing
agent. By nature it is a service company that coordinates and facilitates the logistical flow and processing of products without actually owning a fleet of trucks
or ripening facilities. The company represents the interests of the producers in
the European market.

AgroFair and its producer members foster co-ownership at various levels of
the supply chain. Figure 3 gives an organisational diagram of the ownership
model of AgroFair Europe. The holding AgroFair Europe has three subsidiaries
(in the UK, Benelux and Italy) which provide logistic and marketing support. In
2006, a new subsidiary was set up in the USA (Boston) and country representatives were appointed in Finland and France.

Since Solidaridad established the company in 1996, AgroFair's business
model has built on a number of rationalities. In the first place there was the
economic motive to vertically integrate from primary production to the level of
import and distribution so that producer organisations could gain margins and
value added in the value chain. Besides giving the producer organisations a
better control over year round planning of production and exports, it also gave
them access to profits and dividend payments. Making producers co-owners of
the trade and marketing company AgroFair produced a higher level of commitment between the producers and their first and second level organisations.
And last but not least, by being a producer-owned company, AgroFair managed to attract the specific attention and dedication of several major European
retailers. Some of them (Coop Swiss, Coop UK, Spar, SIWA) adhere to a cooperative business model themselves.

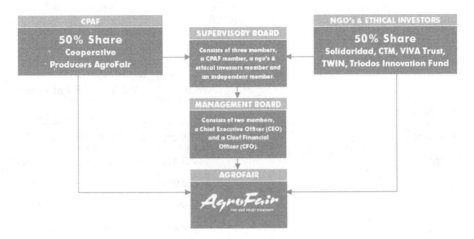

Figure 3. AgroFair's organisational diagram

As stated above the producers collectively own 50% of the holding company's shares which entitles them to 50% of the annual dividends as well as giving them 50% of the votes at the company's board meetings. By maintaining the 50-50 division between the two groups of shareholders, strategic decisions are always made by consensus.

In the international producer cooperative CPAF the voting rights are based on two main principles:

- fifty percent of the voting rights are based on the one-man-one-vote principle;
- fifty percent of the voting rights are allocated on the basis of the FOB value of the traded fruit volumes.

Table 2 shows the division of voting rights according to the traded fruit value and one-man-one-vote principle in 2005.

The producer members of CPAF define their own criteria for membership. The basic criteria include the compliance with the standards of the Fair Trade Labeling Organisation (FLO), which is the international accredited standard setting and inspection body for fair trade standards. In addition, the members themselves also prioritize co-ownership, as well as having a fair say in the management of the production and trade processes. Many of the current members of CPAF are producer organisations that have cooperative or association structures.

By including new fruit categories new organisational modalities have entered the CPAF cooperative. An interesting example of a new CPAF member is Zebediela Citrus Estate, a South African citrus plantation under the Land Reform and Broad-based Black Economic Empowerment program. The Land Reform Program

Table 2. Voting rights for CPAF members in 2006

	FOB Value		
	Average	Member VOTE	Total Vote
Bananas			
Ecuador	53,92%	7,69%	30,80%
Costa Rica	17,74%	7,69%	12,72%
Ghana	6,79%	7,69%	7,23%
Peru	8,97%	7,69%	8,33%
Dominican Republic	0,94%	7,69%	4,32%
Dominican Republic	0,72%	7,69%	4,21%
Mangoes			
Mexico	0,77%	7,69%	4,23%
Burkina Fasso	0,39%	7,69%	4,04%
Burkina Fasso	0,44%	7,69%	4,07%
Peru	0,43%	7,69%	4,06%
Citrus			
South Africa	0,60%	7,69%	4,15%
Argentina	0,15%	7,69%	3,92%
Pineapple			
Costa Rica	8,14%	7,69%	7,92%
	100,00%	100,00%	100,00%

of the South African government has three main sub programs – Restitution, Redistribution and Tenure. It has as a strategic objective to transform the South African Apartheid regime and to create an enabling environment for political, social and economic empowerment of Historically Disadvantaged Individuals. (Historically Disadvantaged Individuals (HDI) refer to any person, category of persons or community that is disadvantaged by unfair discrimination before the Constitution of the Republic of South Africa, 1993. 'Black people' is a generic term including Africans, Coloureds and Indians.) Broad-based Black Economic Empowerment (equitable access and participation) in agriculture means economic empowerment of all black people including women, workers, youth, the disabled and people living in rural areas, through diverse but integrated social or economic strategies that include but are not limited to:

a) Increasing the number of black people that manage, own, and control enterprises and productive assets;

b) Facilitating ownership and management of enterprises and productive assets by black communities, workers, cooperatives and other collective enterprises;

c) Human resource and skills development of black people;

d) Achieving equitable representation in all agricultural professions, occupational categories and levels in the workforce;

e) Preferential procurement; and

f) Investment in enterprises that are owned or managed by black people.

The Zebediela Estate is one of the largest land restitution farms in South Africa. The farm covers about 2000 ha. but forms part of a total land restitution program of 80,000 ha., including a game reserve and several dams (water reservoirs). In October 2003 the farm was restored to its original landowners who were forcefully removed from the land by the Apartheid government some 90 years ago. The farm land now belongs to the surrounding community and workers. The operational company, Zebediela Citrus Estate, is well known all over the world. The farm used to be the largest citrus farm in the Southern Hemisphere, but due to mismanagement and drought the farm went from exporting 2 million cartons in the late 1970s to exporting nothing in 2000. Under serious restructuring and empowerment the farm was able to turn around exporting 300,000 cartons in 2002 and 800,000 cartons in 2003. Destination countries include Russia, the Middle East countries and Japan. The revival of the operational company was possible only by the involvement of a private investment group which started to provide management expertise and injected fresh capital. The Boyes Group acquired 51% of the shares in the operational company with a business model that they called the South Africa Farm Management model (SAFM). The community holds 35% and the workers hold 14% of the shares of the operational company. In a period of 15 years the management and ownership of the company will gradually be handed over to the workers and the community. Figure 4 presents a schematic overview of the South Africa Farm Management model.

Each stakeholder has a complementary role to play: the community contributes the land and facilitates the operational company to expand its business, the workers provide their labour and expertise, and the strategic partners of SAFM provide technical know-how, access to capital, access to markets, and last but not least management skills.

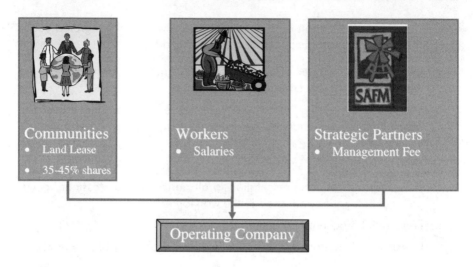

Figure 4. The South African Farm Management model

4 Lessons learned and transferability of the AgroFair model

4.1 Dilemmas in fostering ownership in the fair trade business model

The previous sections have shown that co-ownership and having a joint say in the value export chains is one of the pillars of AgroFair's overall business model. Nevertheless, capacity building among individual producers and their producer organisations to enhance and manage co-ownership has proven to be far from easy. This section presents several of the challenges in fostering ownership in the fair trade business model.

First, the logic of collective action is not always self-evident to individual producers. There is a tension between the self-interest of the individual farmer and that of the collectively owned producer organisation (cooperative or association). Although the sense of ownership between members and their organisation clearly exists, the individual's short-term interest in deriving improved incomes from the cooperative is often bigger than the interest in making long-term investments in the cooperative. Re-investing profits into the growth of the producer organisation competes with a better price or dividend paid to the members. This makes a lot of the primary producer organisations financially weak. Therefore it is even more difficult to make these weak primary organisations co-owners of a secondary organisation that is shareholder in a European based import company.

Second, it is difficult to advise, let alone prescribe, specific organisational modalities of co-ownership. As there is a large range of business models, such

as cooperatives, associations, limited liability companies, there is no single op-
timal design. Agricultural producers lack the training and capacity to assess the
various modalities and decide what suits their specific situation and circumstances best. For the purpose of certification FLO distinguishes only between
producer groups or associations and large-scale plantations that operate as
private enterprises and mainly work with hired labour force.

The fair trade movement, as well as the CPAF, discuss an ideal producer
profile within the fair trade movement vigorously. There is a serious concern
that FLO policy makers and other stakeholders will make the size of farms
(surface in hectares) a binding criterion for eligibility for certification. Instead
of using compliance with the social code of conduct (or the degree of control
and co-ownership) as standard criteria, steps have been taken to define number of hectares as the main indicator of whether a farm can or cannot be certified. A real-life example of this criterion is the newly defined fair trade (FLO)
standard for Brazil. FLO has limited the access for Brazilian fruit plantations
that employ hired labour setting down the following criteria for the period
from 1 July, 2006 to 30 June, 2008 (see Annex 1): a) Limitation of the size of
land to four fiscal or cadastral entities (módulos fiscais) (5 to 100 hectares
per modulo depending on the region); b) The owner and/or family members
is/are directly involved in the management of the unit in question; and c) The
owner lives on the unit in question or nearby. Setting a maximum farm size is
conflicting with the original development objective of giving smallholder producers access to export markets: how can they grow if FLO sets maximum
sizes for their farms?

Third, the AgroFair experience shows that it is difficult to unite producer
organisations of various fruit categories and countries of origin in one producer-owned business concept. The diversity of AgroFair members/shareholders
has grown considerably over the past 10 years. The commercial volumes of
main products like banana and citrus contrast enormously with the lesser fruit
categories like mango. This leads to unequal political weight in CPAF. The
fact that some fruit categories are produced year-round (banana, pineapple),
while others are seasonal (mango with a three-month season per year) reflects a completely different relation between the farmers and their cooperative. The seasonal nature of mango requires sourcing from multiple climate
regions resulting in a partner portfolio of Spanish, French, English and Portu-
guese speaking producer organisations. AgroFair Europe faces the logistical
and organisational dilemma of a multinational company when choosing language and translations for its shareholder meetings. The minimum cost of a
shareholder meeting is EUR 50,000, which is mainly spent on travel expendi-
tures to bring producers from various countries to one single spot.

Fourth, the representatives of the producer organisations that are a member
of the AgroFair family face the challenge of strengthening their capacity as co-

operative managers, cooperative board members, and shareholders in Agro-Fair Europe. By being a producer and at the same time being directly involved in the management of the cooperative or board member of an operational company there is a serious risk of conflicting interests. It requires a high level of professionalism to separate the various interests one person has to defend. Making a clear division between the tasks and responsibilities of the management and the board of the producer organisation is an important step towards professionalisation.

Fifth, mention should be made of the fact that AgroFair has been aware of a number of the above-mentioned needs for capacity building. In 2002 a specific instrument was created to promote organisational and institutional capacity building of producer organisations. Based on a strategic agreement between two Dutch donor organisations, ICCO and Solidaridad, the AgroFair Assistance & Development Foundation (AFAD) was created. This foundation provides assistance in a number of areas: organisational development, quality assurance & certification, access to finance, and access to markets. Focus has been on solving the day-to-day challenges to maintain or gain producer positions in the market. At the same time it has become clear that promoting organisational development takes time! The 15-year time frame that Zebediela has defined for developing a new generation of plantation managers seems far more realistic than the one to three-year time frame that many donor programs use for obtaining results in producer organization development.

Finally, the involvement of the NGO's and ethical foundations in AgroFair's strategy through their financial investment ensures a sound balance of the three aspects of the triple bottom-line; profit, people and planet. Being deeply involved in the sustainable agenda of the countries these NGOs originate from, their insights in consumer perception and values are valuable for AgroFair. These insights are regularly shared within the market development team leading to an ongoing discussion of the producer organisation and consumer communication.

A good example is AgroFair's cooperation with TWIN. AgroFair and TWIN set up AgroFair UK to introduce fair trade fruit in the UK market. TWIN seeks to use trade to positively redress unequal relations between North and South, to build better livelihoods for the poorest and the most marginalised in the trading chain and to promote developmental and longer term improvement in the political and economic environment. In Italy AgroFair established a similar partnership with CTM resulting in the joint venture CTM-AgroFair. The main objective of these subsidiaries is market development. It also reflects AgroFair's vision of being close to producers and consumers in order to maintain competitive advantage.

5   The mainstreaming of fair trade as a new challenge for AgroFair

While fair trade originally only attracted the attention of smallholder producer organisations that operated in a niche market, in the past two years main fruit operators like Dole and Capespan have entered the fair trade fruit arena with the aim to serve the mainstream market. The launch of fair trade products by mainstream multinational food retail companies (like Coop, Aldi, Lidl, Wal-Mart, and others) has been dismissed by some as the cynical exploitation of ethical consumerism.[1] But the fact that fair trade is now attracting such interest underlines consumers' growing interest in ethical concerns.[2]

In numerical terms, the market may still be classified as a niche but the days when this area was dominated by marginal producers and alternative trade organisations are long gone. And it is perhaps a testament to the success of those early pioneers and campaigners that mainstream operators such as Cadbury Schweppes, Kraft and Nestlé are now showing interest in this segment of the market. According to a recent report on ethical consumerism, labelled fair trade products generated an estimated USD100 million in additional producers' income in 2004, thanks to an estimated USD 1 billion in global retail sales of all fair trade goods.[3] This represents a 49-% increase over the previous year.

---

[1]   In June 2006 LIDL launched a fair trade line in Germany named 'Fairglobe'. In co-operation with the national fair trade initiative Transfair the discount retailer started to offer roast coffee, bananas and other food products that are sourced at a guaranteed minimum price in order to support small farmers in Latin America. However, Transfair's cooperation with the discount chain has already been criticised by people close to Transfair as Lidl is "renowned for social dumping". Apart from the new fair trade line, Lidl in Germany launched its 'Bioness' organic private label range. (www.planetretail.net Daily News 19 April 2006).

[2]   December 2006 witnessed the world's biggest conversion of its kind; Sainsbury's announced that it would be the first UK retailer to convert its entire banana range to fair trade. The retail price of bananas will remain unchanged. The move provides unprecedented volume to fair trade sales and will make Sainsbury's share of the entire fair trade market larger than all the other major supermarkets in the UK combined. Sainsbury's is already the UK's leading fair trade retailer and accounts for the largest market share of bananas with the fair trade label. As a result of converting to 100 % fair trade, Sainsbury's will buy five times as many fair trade bananas. This conversion will create a social premium of GBP 4 million in 2007, which will be returned to the growers and their communities. This is an increase of over GBP 3 m in 2006. Sainsbury's CEO Justin King said: "This move to 100 per cent fair trade leads the world, and really sets the standard for global fair trade sourcing."

[3]   "Global market review of fair trade and ethical food – forecasts to 2012", at www.just-food.com

Moreover, the increasing involvement of large mainstream companies is likely to signal an acceleration of this growth.

In November 2006, a spokesperson from Kraft Foods, the world's second largest food company, predicted that within the next decade, 60% to 80% of the coffee market will be taken up by products with independent certification for fair trade issues. Cadbury Schweppes' acquisition of leading fair trade and organic chocolate company Green & Black's has prompted speculation that future merger and acquisition activities will focus on grabbing a share of the ethical market. Large multinationals such as Cadbury can increase their profits, and their ethical reputation, through the acquisition of a smaller, established, ethical company. L'Oreal's acquisition of the Body Shop is a non-food example of this trend.

Skeptics argue that large companies such as Nestlé view ethical consumerism as the next marketing buzzword, a trend that is worthy of investment. But what is clear is that fair trade as an idea has moved on considerably since it was first introduced in the Netherlands more than 20 years ago. The major driver behind the development of the ethical and fair trade market is information. Consumers in many countries worldwide are now aware of the unfair treatment of developing world producers, and are keen to show their support by purchasing the occasional fair trade product. Consumers want to see companies becoming more ethical, caring and compassionate about the product, the consumer, the world we live in, and the environment.

The arrival of multinational companies in the fair trade arena might again threaten to push the smallholder cooperatives out of the international retail market. Lower prices will be the inevitable result when these companies aim for an increase in demand for fair trade products. It is believed that this will have a negative, long-term impact on the producers. Again, economies of scale principles will put smaller producers at a disadvantage. This raises the ultimate question what will be the unique selling point of smallholder producer organisations when the fair trade label on their product is no longer unique?

References

Nicholls A. and C. Opal (2004). *Fair Trade market driven ethical consumption*. Sage Publications ltd, London,

Arias P., Dankers, C., Lui, P., and P. Pilkauskas (2003). *The world banana economy 1985 – 2002* (FAO), Rome.

Codron, J.-M., Sirieix, L. and T. Reardon (2006). Social and environmental attributes of food products in an emerging mass market: Challenges of signalling and consumer perception. *Agriculture and Human Values, 23* (3) Fall Issue. Pp. 283-297.

Meer, C.L.J. van der (2006). Exclusion of small-scale farmers from coordinated supply chains. Market failure, policy failure or just economies of scale?. In: R. Ruben, M. Slingerland and H. Nijhoff (Eds.), *Agro-food chains and networks for development*. Springer, 209-217. Wageningen.

Klein, N. (1999). *No Logo*, St Martin's Press, Picador, New York USA.

Reardon, T. (2006). The rapid rise of supermarkets and the use of private standards in their food procurement systems in developing countries. In: R. Ruben, M. Slingerland and H. Nijhoff (Eds.), *Agro-food chains and networks for development*, Springer, pp. 79-105.

Roozen, N. and F. van der Hoff (2003) *Fair Trade*. Van Gennep, Amsterdam

Websites

www.agrofair.nl
www.solidaridad.nl
www.fairtrade.net

A Management Model for Sustainability in the Financial Sector

The case of Banco Real

Christel Scholten

Abstract. Since 1998, Banco Real, the third largest private bank in Brazil, has relentlessly worked to create a 'new bank for a new society', by integrating social, environmental and economic aspects into the business. Its management model was adopted in 2001, evolved in 2006 and is used to guide the organisation towards achieving its ambitious vision and mission. The model focuses the organisation on creating sustainable results by creating value for and contributing to the total satisfaction of the organisation's key stakeholders – employees, clients, suppliers, shareholders, society and the environment. The individual is at the centre of the model because of a strong belief that each individual plays a role as a change agent in contributing to the evolution of society. The case of Banco Real demonstrates that the integration of sustainability into its model is a win-win-win strategy for shareholders, clients, employees and other stakeholders.

Key words: sustainable development, financial sector, governance, integration into core business, stakeholders

1 Introduction and background of the company

Until 2007, Banco Real was part of the ABN AMRO Group which began its operations in Brazil in 1917 as Banco Holandês da America do Sul. Banco Real, a retail bank, has been active in Brazil since 1971 and was acquired by the ABN AMRO Group in 1998. Since 1998, Banco Real has acquired two other Brazilian banks, Bandepe and Sudameris and in addition to managing operations in Brazil, gained the responsibility for the Latin American operations of the ABN AMRO Group at the beginning of 2006. In Brazil, Banco Real has 33,000 employees, over 13 million clients, 2000 branches and banking service points, approximately 1,400 suppliers, many strategic partners and supports approximately 60 local community organisations. Banco Real consists of wholesale and retail banking operations, Asset Management, Private Banking, micro credit and a consumer finance business. Brazil is a competitive financial market with several national banks competing for market share including Itaú, Bradesco, Banco do Brasil, Caixa Econômica Federal and Unibanco. The other major international banks operating in Brazil include Citigroup, HSBC and Santander which acquired Banco Real in 2007.

While Banco Real was part of the ABN AMRO Group, it adopted the Group´s values and Business Principles. Group wide, ABN AMRO's values were launched in 1997 and were adopted by the organisation in Brazil during the integration. The corporate values are: integrity, respect, teamwork and professionalism. To further clarify ABN AMRO's values, business principles were later introduced to serve as a compass for the organisation.

ABN AMRO business principles

1. Employees are the Heart of our Organisation

2. Employees Pursue Excellence

3. The Organisation Aims to Maximise Long-term Shareholder Value

4. The Organisation Manages Risk Prudently and Professionally

5. The Organisation Strives to Provide Excellent Service

6. The Organisation Builds its Business on Confidentiality

7. The Organisation Assesses Business Partners on their Standards

8. The Organisation is a Responsible Institution and a Good Corporate Citizen

9. The Organisation Respects Human Rights and the Environment

10. The Organisation is Accountable for its Actions and is Open About Them

The values were introduced into the organisation in Brazil through a launch at an annual meeting of managers in 1999. They were then cascaded throughout the organisation through a communication campaign and sessions led by managers using an interactive game and exercises. The Business Principles were introduced in Brazil in 2005, when copies were distributed to all employees, reinforcing Banco Real's position in sustainable development.

2   History of the management model

From the beginning, when Fabio C. Barbosa assumed leadership of the newly acquired organisation as President in 1998, he declared that the organisation needed to create a *'new bank for a new society'*, integrating social, environmental and economic dimensions into all aspects of the business. *"We need to influence capitalism to become more humane and inclusive."* In a country with glaring income disparity and rapidly depleting natural resources, the private sector plays an extremely important role in creating a model that incorporates wider societal concerns. Despite ranking 10th in 2006[1] in terms of GDP, Brazil, a country with a population of 184 million[2], ranks 70th [3] on the Human Development Index (HDI) and 116th [4] on the UN Gini Index, an income inequality metric. In terms of the environment, Brazil loses significant amounts of its forests to deforestation each year and air, soil and water pollution is on an increase. The challenges are significant, and too great for the government to handle alone, requiring the leadership of the private sector to set an example and create innovative solutions.

The starting point of the management model was a conviction that the bank should be based on relationships which set the tone for the future inclusion of a wider group of stakeholders. In 2000, the vision for the organisation was created: *"The Brazilian market and society are evolving and require a new role for banks. Banks should act as facilitators of a society that is economically efficient, socially just, politically democratic and environmentally sustainable. We desire this change and aim to be one of the leaders of this transition in the market and in society."*

In 2001, the organisation's mission and model were created. With the acquisition of Banco Real by ABN AMRO Bank, Fabio Barbosa saw the opportunity to create a new type of model. Rather than hiring a consultancy to facilitate the process, the president led brainstorming sessions with a group of executives to discuss what a new bank for a new society meant in practice. From these discussions the mission and model emerged. The mission: *To satisfy the client, creating value for shareholders, employees and the community, maintaining the highest standards of ethics, and differentiating ourselves by the quality of our products, services and, most importantly, exemplary client servicing,* clearly

---

[1]   World Bank 2006 GDP Ranking.
      Source: http://siteresources.worldbank.org/DATASTATISTICS/Resources
[2]   In 04/01/2007, there were 183,989,711 inhabitants in Brazil, according to population counting realized by IBGE (Brazilian Institute of Geography and Statistics). Source: www.ibge.gov.br
[3]   Human Development Index 2005. Source: http://hdr.undp.org
[4]   United Nations Development Program 2007/2008 Human Development Report. Source: http://hdrstats.undp.org/indicators

states the organisation's commitment to creating value in an ethical way for shareholders and a wider group of stakeholders.

The focus of the model is on creating totally satisfied clients achieving this through four pillars: focus on the client's focus, skilled and engaged staff, competitive tools and corporate values. This focus contributes to creating results for shareholders, employees and the community.

Figure 1. Banco Real management model 2001-2006

The essence of the strategy of the organisation is to grow and to increase its value through attracting and retaining clients, increasing employee engagement and satisfaction and positioning itself as a leader in governance, ethics and sustainability.

From the beginning, sustainable development was a core aspect of the organisation's strategy. Three principles that are important for the organisation on this journey are:

1. interdependency

2. change from within

3. the triple bottom line (considering people, planet and profit).

Interdependency: The organisation sees itself as part of a web of relationships with other players including clients, suppliers, shareholders, the government, the community, employees, the environment and the media, among others. By being aware of these relationships and engaging with these players, the organisation can better understand their needs and aspirations, can develop better strategies, products and processes and can work together to create a better society.

Change from Within: The movement started as an organic process and each initiative begins by raising awareness among and engaging employees who then influence practices within the organisation. The practices the organisation adopts influence change in the market with clients, suppliers, partners and competitors which then have a wider impact on society and the environment.

Triple Bottom Line: The organisation is committed to integrating the three Ps or People, Planet and Profit dimensions into all aspects of the organisation and into all business decisions.

During the same year that the mission and model had been defined, the Bank of Value Committee was formed. This committee of senior leaders of the organisation discussed in more depth strategies for becoming a new bank for a new society. A number of ideas were generated during these committee meetings which were followed up on by groups of employees that were set up to take responsibility for the further development and implementation of these ideas. These groups include the environment, diversity and suppliers *frentes* (fronts) while other groups were set up to create the ethical fund, micro credit and risk policy. At the end of 2001, the Social Responsibility Department, reporting directly to the President, was set up to coordinate the integration of sustainable development into the organisation with the clear intention from the beginning to dissolve within the next few years to ensure this integration.

In 2002, three committees were set up, the Market, Management and Social Action Committees, providing forums for participants to discuss and further develop ideas for the different streams of sustainable development. Many of the initiatives that exist today emerged from the discussions during the meetings held by the committees and groups set up in 2001 and 2002. The Market Committee discussed projects and ideas related to the core business such as the ethical fund, micro credit, the social and environmental risk process, sustainability products, and engagement of clients in sustainability. The Management Committee discussed projects and ideas related to internal management such as diversity, eco-efficiency and suppliers, and the Social Action Committee discussed the social investment strategy and projects to focus on and invest in.

A key aspect that the organisation believes contributes to its gaining of credibility in sustainability is that it integrates sustainability into its core business such as the creation of a social and environmental risk filter for the extension of credit to corporate clients, the development of social and environmental financial products including lines of credit for social and environmental improvements, technologies and innovations, the ethical fund and the creation of new businesses such as micro credit for low income populations. In addition to integrating sustainability into its core business, the organisation has also developed initiatives which other companies in other industries could also adopt such as a diversity program, eco-efficiency initiatives, education and training on sustainability, engagement of suppliers in sustainability issues, communications and social investment.

In 2003, the Social Responsibility Department temporarily merged with the training academy to form the Education and Sustainable Development (ESD)

Table 1. Location and transfer of sustainability initiatives in Banco Real

Initiative	Location	Year	Transferred to/Set up in department	Year
Ethical Fund	Asset Management	2001	Asset Management	2001
Engagement with Suppliers	Social Responsibility/ ESD	2001	Group Finance/ Procurement	2004
Social and Environment Risk Policy	Working Group	2002	Risk Department	2002
Microcredit	Social Responsibility/ ESD	2002	Risk Department (temporarily until transferred to a business line)	2005
Social and Environmental Products			Products Department	2003
Social and Environmental Product Sales	Products Department	2003	Product Sales	2005
Eco-efficiency	Working Group	2001	Infrastructure and Logistics	2006
Diversity	Working Group	2001	Human Resources	2003
Sustainability Report – content	Social Responsibility/ ESD	2002	Brand Strategy and Corporate Communications Department	2006
Sustainability Indicators	Social Responsibility/ ESD	2002	Group Finance	2006
Education and Training	Social Responsibility/ ESD	2003	Human Resources	2006
Sustainable Construction			Engineering Department	2006

Department. This strategic decision was made based on the belief that education is one of the best ways to integrate sustainable development in the organisation. After a period of three years, the training and education department returned to Human Resources – with sustainable development now permeating the education model and the majority of the courses the organisation offers.

From the beginning, it was very clear that the Social Responsibility/Education and Sustainable Development Department would not be a fixed structure in the organisation. It would be a flexible structure that would change and evolve based on the needs of the organisation and trends in society. Many initiatives were initially housed in the department, which served as an incubator, and then later were transferred to another department. Other initiatives were incorporated by the department for a temporary period, such as the training academy, until it was felt that sustainability was reasonably integrated to be able to return to its original owner. It is very important for the department not be become attached to a particular initiative or project as when the time is right, it will be returned to or transferred to an appropriate department in the organisation. At the same time, units of sustainability were set up in existing departments such as a social and environmental risk unit in the risk department, a social and environmental products unit in the products department, and a social and environmental product sales unit in the sales department. Examples of this process are described in table 1.

In addition to incubating new initiatives and temporarily housing initiatives or projects from other departments, one of the core activities of the department is to oversee the strategy for and governance of sustainable development in the organisation and to support departments in the integration of sustainable development into their respective strategies, businesses, processes, policies, training programs and relationships with stakeholders.

3   Governance of and strategy for sustainable development

Banco Real's overall strategic objective for sustainable development is to integrate sustainability into all strategies, products, processes, policies and relationships of the organisation. This objective is facilitated primarily by two things, the evolution of the governance model for sustainability and through supporting each department in integrating sustainability into their respective core businesses.

In 2005, the leaders of the sustainability movement in the organisation recognized that it was no longer necessary to maintain separate committees to discuss the integration of sustainable development. The Management and Market Committees ceased to exist while the Social Investment Committee was maintained as the function it held was still relevant. A formal governance model was set up having as its primary objective the development and management of the organisation's sustainability strategy and accountability for its sustainability performance.

In May 2006, as part of the evolution of the governance model, Banco Real set up a Sustainability Council. The Council meets once a month and its membership includes 30 senior leaders from the majority of the organisation's departments. The Council is chaired by the President and several executive directors are members, demonstrating a very high level of commitment from the leadership of the organisation. The objectives of the Sustainability Council include:

- Ensuring the management of and accountability for sustainability including the development and management of the sustainability strategy;
- Ensuring the transition of responsibility accountability for the integration of sustainability to the individual departments of the organisation; and
- Guaranteeing and monitoring the sustainability performance of the organisation.

The Sustainability Council monitors the sustainability action plans for each department, overall sustainability indicators for the organisation, performance of the competition in sustainability and debates and approves strategic projects. Below is a list of the key sustainability performance indicators that are monitored:

- Business generated through Social and Environmental Products
- Business generated through operations that address sustainability issues (social, environmental, economic)
- Business generated from clients that were positively screened through the social and environmental risk questionnaire
- Business generated through the Ethical Fund
- Business generated through Micro credit
- Business generated through Carbon Credit financing
- Client loyalty
- Ranking of the sustainable development brand attribute (comparison with peers)
- Number of times mentioned in the media on sustainability
- Number of awards received in sustainability

- Number of clients that received training or participated in forums on sustainability organized by Banco Real
- Number of suppliers that received training or participated in forums on sustainability organized by Banco Real
- Number of social and environmental risk analyses conducted
- Number of branches and administrative buildings with recycling facilities
- CO_2 emissions
- Water consumption
- Energy consumption
- Paper consumption
- Toner consumption
- Employee Engagement Index
- Employee turnover
- Employee lawsuits against Banco Real
- Number of employees trained in sustainable development
- Employee participation in social investment projects sponsored by Banco Real

All of the departments of the organisation have a sustainability action plan. These departments include: Wholesale (large companies), Middle (medium-sized companies), Treasury, Products, Segments, Channels, Private Banking, Retail (Consumer and Corporate Clients), Real Estate, Micro credit, Shared Services and Operations, Consumer Finance, Asset Management, Finance, Risk, Human Resources, Legal, Marketing, Security, Audit and Compliance. During a Council meeting in March 2007, 25 plans were presented. Each plan included how the department aims to maintain competitiveness through integrating sustainability into its core business, processes and policies, through the education and engagement of employees, and the engagement of clients, suppliers and other stakeholders. Plans for new products and innovations in processes were also presented. In 2007 a team of individuals in the Sustainable Development Department was trained and uses a methodology developed by the organisation to support departments in further integrating sustainability.

The governance model for sustainability and the strategy for integrating sustainability into the core business of each department partly address the difficulties faced in engaging senior leaders, including the more sceptical ones, and integrating sustainability into all strategies, processes, products and relationships of the organisation. By working closely with and raising awareness of sustainability among leaders in each department, and linking the integration of sustainability with the strategy and core business of the department, leaders are increasingly coming on board. During the meetings of the Sustainability Council it became apparent which departments were more engaged and which were not as engaged, creating internal pressure on those not yet engaged. Whereas early on it was more difficult to engage senior leaders, today the tables have turned and some senior leaders are even requesting to be part of the Council. The Council has created accountability for sustainability, decentralized responsibilities to the departments and created more transparency and awareness within the organisation.

One of the key challenges is to continue to further align and integrate the sustainability plans and targets of each department into its regular business plans and targets. Another is to ensure further alignment between the overall sustainability targets and indicators and the corporate strategy. Sustainability strategies, targets and indicators should not be parallel to those of the organisation but should be completely integrated. One of the ways these challenges are being addressed is through the integration of sustainability into the strategic planning process of the organisation which was developed and implemented in 2007. Guidelines including sustainability criteria along four dimensions (core business, policies and processes, training and engagement of staff and stakeholder relationships) were developed and integrated into the overall strategic planning process of the organisation and into the specific planning processes of the departments.

4   Evolution of the management model

At the end of 2006, at an annual gathering of 600 managers, the organisation's revised vision, mission and model were launched. These were updated to better reflect the organisation's beliefs – that everything is interconnected and that we are part of a web of diverse stakeholders, that we need to incorporate social, environmental and economic aspects into all business decisions, and that we should aim for the satisfaction of the individual, regardless of the relationship that a person has with the organisation – whether he or she is a client, supplier, part of the community, shareholder or employee.

The revised vision is: *A new bank for a new society. A society in evolution, increasingly better informed and aware, strives to integrate human, environmental and economic aspects in all of its decisions. We, as an organisation and as individuals are change agents in this evolution.* As an organisation and as individuals we believe that we are change agents and have a role to play in contributing to the evolution of society. We are aware of the shift in consciousness of society and strive to be leaders of the movement particularly in Brazil.

The revised mission is: *To be an organisation renowned for providing outstanding financial services to our clients, achieving sustainable results and the satisfaction of individuals and organisations, who together with us contribute to the evolution of society.* We aim to provide high quality services and make a profit but not at all costs. We aim to generate results sustainably, by integrating the social, environmental and economic aspects into all that we do. We strive for the satisfaction of individuals and organisations and invite them to join us on our journey to create a sounder society.

Our Model

Figure 2. Banco Real management model 2006

In the evolution of the model, the individual is the focus in the centre. We aim to show that each individual can play more than one role. At the same time that one is a client, one could also be a mother or father, be involved in an environmental organisation and be on a council of the municipal government, a citizen of society.

With this model we aim to create value for our key stakeholders – employees, clients, suppliers, shareholders, society and the environment, contributing to their total satisfaction. We want to engage with our stakeholders as we believe that together we can work towards the sustainability of our society. The four pillars have evolved slightly, now based on: shared values, focus on the client's focus, engagement, and processes and discipline. We believe that this together contributes to the achievement of sustainable results.

The choice to include sustainable development in our overall management model is due to a deep belief that this will enable us to live our mission and achieve our vision. We believe that we are a successful organisation because we have adopted practices that integrate the social, environmental and economic dimensions into our day-to-day operations, aspects that society is increasingly valuing. The integration of sustainable development contributes to the realization of the strategic objectives of the organisation by improving results, attracting and retaining clients, increasing employee engagement and satisfaction and putting the organisation in a leadership position in governance, ethics and sustainability. *"The whole sustainability strategy is a win-win-win proposition, where shareholders, clients, employees and other stakeholders get good results,"* President Fabio Barbosa remarks.

In practice the integration of sustainable development into our model means that social, environmental and economic aspects are integrated into the overall strategy of the organisation and the strategies and plans of each area of the organisation, whether it be a business unit such as retail banking or a support function such as human resources. It is a new way of looking at the business.

In the **business functions**, the focus is more on engaging clients, understanding not only their financial needs but also their environmental and social needs. For example a client may want to reduce the amount of contaminated water that enters the river from the company´s factory. Banco Real can offer a line of credit to install a water treatment and recycling system. In addition to reducing negative environmental impacts, the installation of new technology can also reduce the client's costs by reducing water consumption contributing to greater profitability of the client's operations. For the business functions, the focus is also on developing and offering new and innovative products which provide environmental and social solutions for our clients. For the **support and back office functions**, the focus is more on integrating social and environmental aspects into core processes such as the remuneration and incentive systems, internal and external communications and processes dealing with the use of environmental resources such as energy, water, paper and building materials. For **employees** overall, sustainability can be applied in their day-to day-activities such as use of energy, water, paper, proper recycling and destination of waste, embracing diversity, engaging with suppliers, clients and the wider community around the topic, getting involved in volunteer activities and being proactive by questioning practices, policies and processes that are not consistent with sustainable development. Many employees also bring these concepts into their personal lives by reducing the use of natural resources, implementing recycling systems in their houses or apartment buildings, getting involved in volunteer activities and in general creating awareness around sustainability.

Along this journey to become a new bank for a new society, a number of results have been achieved. This next section will describe these in more detail. We believe that the efforts in sustainable development all contribute to creating sustainable results. These results include increased revenues, increased number of clients that bank with us because of our commitment to sustainable development, new products that meet the environmental and social needs of our clients, increased brand attractiveness, integration of sustainable development into our processes reducing risks and costs for the organisation, attraction of foreign capital, increased employee satisfaction and engagement, increased diversity in the organisation, reduction of the use of natural resources therefore reducing costs, and increased engagement with our stakeholders which attracts more people to the organisation and contributes to an improved positioning in the market.

While difficult to directly attribute results to one of the four pillars of the model: focus on the client's focus, shared values, engaged employees, and improved processes and discipline, the results will be framed around one or two of the pillars.

Focus on the client's focus and sustainable results. Through its results, Banco Real is demonstrating that sustainability contributes to financial performance. Since the year 2000, Banco Real's net profit has grown from USD 159 million to USD 1.7 billion in 2007 and revenues have also increased, from USD 5.6 billion in 2002 to 7.2 billion in 2007. The number of clients that bank with the organisation increased from 4.8 million in 2000 to 13.1 million in 2006. Results from Client Satisfaction Surveys by The Gallup Organization show that the number of clients that recommend the bank has grown from 34% in 2002 to 44% in 2006 and that client satisfaction has also increased during the same period from 68% to 74%. In a ranking of Brazilian brands by the Magazine *Isto É Dinheiro* in partnership with BrandAnalytics, Banco Real´s brand ranked 9th, valued at USD 384 million. The 119% increase of Banco Real´s brand from 2005 to 2006 was the largest yearly increase among the 18 most valuable brand names listed. The magazine stated that the increased value of Banco Real´s brand reflects the organization´s consistent positioning in sustainability. *"Business clients, both small and large companies, are now taking our stance into consideration and have either intensified their business or started doing business with us. Many have stated explicitly that they did this because of what we stand for. Our brand has moved up from fifth to second place and has maintained this position since 2005 in terms of brand attractiveness and recognition (among other banks). This means that when individuals are asked in a survey which bank they would open an account with, we rank second,"* says Fabio Barbosa.

In terms of innovation in products and offerings to clients, contributing to increased results, Banco Real was the first bank in Latin America to launch an Ethical Fund. This fund was the world's best performer in Socially Responsible Investing (SRI) in 2004 and its portfolio grew from USD 25.1 million in 2004 to USD 434 million in 2007. Accumulated growth since its inception in 2001 to the end of 2007 was 504.5% while the accumulated growth of the São Paulo Stock Exchange Index (Ibovespa) during this same period was 418.2%. The organisation also created new business and closed new deals with the new line of social and environmental products. Credit that was extended for social and environmental projects for both consumer and corporate clients reached USD 466 million in 2007. An example of a social and environmental operation is the deal with Votorantim Celulose e Papel (VCP), a pulp and paper company. In an innovative partnership between VCP and Banco Real, the Poupança Florestral Programme was created, in which agricultural producers, members of the landless movement, received credit from Banco Real at lower rates to sustainably grow eucalyptus trees on a reserved part of their land. This partnership protects the forests, guarantees production for VCP and income for the members of the landless movement. In another innovative partnership between Banco Real, Tetrapak, Klabin (a pulp and paper company) and Alcoa, the organisation extended financing for the implementation of a new technology that separates the aluminium, paper and plastic from Tetrapak containers. The separated material is used as raw material for the production processes of the partner companies. The organisation is a pioneer in Brazil in investing in renewable technology and arranging carbon credit deals bringing business and value to the organisation. Up to 2006, the organisation financed 20 small hydroelectric plants with a total generation capacity of 423 MW, four wind farms with a total generation capacity of 199 MW and two bio diesel plants. This contributed to the direct and indirect generation of 70,000 jobs, is a significant investment in infrastructure for the country and generates profit in fees for the bank. In 2006, Banco Real conducted EUR 9.7 million in carbon credit trades.

Banco Real was also a pioneer in micro credit. The number of clients grew from 579 in 2003 to 53,421 in 2007 with a total disbursed value of USD 32 million in 26 communities. The break-even point was reached in November 2007. Because of its credibility and diligence with social and environmental issues, Banco Real gained long-term international capital, receiving a total of USD 324 million from the International Finance Corporation (IFC) since 2004 for a social and environmental and corporate governance credit line. A significant contributor to the results of the organisation is positive media exposure which attracts clients and other stakeholders to the organisation.

Improved processes and discipline. Banco Real was the first bank in the region to create a social and environmental risk process, reducing the organisation's financial and reputational risk. 3,177 social and environmental risk analyses were conducted in 2006. Since the adoption of the Equator Principles, 24 analyses have been conducted, of which three were rejected. Initiatives on the eco-efficiency front contribute to reducing costs and use of natural resources. 1027 branches have set up recycling facilities whereby the waste is collected by cooperatives. In addition, the organisation was a pioneer in the mass use of recycled paper internally and was the first bank to produce cheque books with recycled paper. Efforts have been made to reduce paper usage, which currently is at approximately 75 kg per employee per year. The car fleet has been renewed, 1659 of which are now dual fuel systems (gasoline and ethanol). In terms of reduction in resource use, the organisation reduced its energy consumption by 4% in 2004 with an additional reduction of 7% in 2005 and a further reduction of 4% in 2006 and 2007. The organisation reduced water consumption by 9% in 2004 with an additional reduction of 3.4% in 2005 and a further reduction of 11% in 2006 and 2007. Up to 2005, this amounts to savings of USD 183,000 in energy and USD 56,000 in water. In 2006, Banco Real received ISO14000 certification for its administrative building in São Paulo and received a silver status certification by the Leadership in Energy and Environmental Design (LEED) Green Building Rating System for its first sustainably built branch.

Engagement. Engaged and satisfied employees contribute to sustainable results. In 2001 the employee satisfaction rate was 68% increasing to 77% in 2003. In 2006, the employee engagement rate was 91% and employee pride in working at Banco Real grew from 92% in 2001 to 98% in 2006. In terms of diversity in the organisation, it witnessed an increase in the number of employees with disabilities from 272 in 2004 to 1369 in 2007 and in the same period, the employees of African descent grew from 9.87% to 14%. The organisation has a target to increase the percentage of women in managerial positions which currently is at 25%.

Banco Real also invests significantly in employee training and since 2002, programs on sustainability have been provided for all levels of the organisation. The first large scale program was run in 2002 in partnership with Friends of the Earth training 1500 retail branch and relationship managers on social and environmental risk. Since then, the number of staff trained has increased and in 2007 alone 12,590 employees were trained on the topic of sustainability. One of the flagship programs in 2007 was the Development of Leaders in Sustainability Program, a program designed to develop leaders in sustainability in the retail branch network across Brazil. Participants in the program become a reference in sustainability in their region, not only for their teams but also for clients, suppliers and the wider community. The program consists of 3 modules for a total of 52 hours in-class training and the 200 participants upon completion of each module cascade the content to a further 2000 managers.

Since 2001, the organisation has increased engagement with its suppliers. Starting with a small group of 15 in 2001, this number has grown to 164 in 2007. 458 have signed the organisation's Value Partnership which includes a set of guidelines for the inclusion of social and environmental considerations into the suppliers' businesses. In 2006, the legal department engaged 100 law firms in sustainable development issues reducing risks and costs for the organisation. The treasury department also began to engage brokerage firms in 2006 to align values and raise awareness about the topic. The organisation also engages clients in sustainable development, raising awareness about the topic and exploring ways in which clients can adopt sustainability practices in their companies. This indirectly leads to increased business and increased client loyalty. With respect to social investment, 4,614 clients and 17,472 employees participated in and donated to the Real Friend Program in 2007, where part of an individuals' taxes can be destined to social projects. Also in 2007, the organisation had 1959 volunteers working on the Brazil School Project, a project focused on education.

Banco Real is beginning to receive recognition for its efforts in sustainability, contributing to the brand value and attractiveness of the organisation. In 2007 alone, ABN AMRO received 35 awards for its performance in sustainable development. A few of the awards and recognition that the organisation has received include:

- Harvard Business School Case – ABN AMRO Real: Banking on Sustainability (2005)
- World Business Awards (2006 – one of 10 companies awarded by the International Chamber of Commerce, UNEP and the Prince of Wales Business Leaders' Forum)
- Emerging Bank of the Year (2006 – Financial Times Sustainable Banking Awards)
- 100 Best Companies to Work For in Brazil (2006 and 2007 – Great Place to Work Institute and Epoca Magazine)
- 100 Best Companies to Work For in Latin America (2004 to 2007 – Great Place to Work Institute and Epoca Magazine)
- 150 Best Companies to Work For in Brazil (2002-2007 – Exame and Você S.A. Magazines)
- One of 20 role model companies in sustainability in Brazil (Guia Exame de Sustentabilidade 2007)
- Prêmio ECO 2007 – awarded the Grand Prize for Management of Sustainability and in 4 other categories: Values, Transparency and Governance; Employees; Suppliers; and Government and Society
- 8th place among the Most Admired Companies in Brazil and 2nd place within the banking sector (2007 – Carta Capital magazine and the TNS InterScience Institute)

Increasingly, Banco Real is being seen as a leader in Brazil and internationally in integrating sustainability into its core business model. Indicators demonstrate that the model is working as the business is growing, results are increasing, more clients are being attracted to the bank, employees are satisfied and engaged and brand and reputation ratings are increasing. The integration of sustainability into the core business is proving to be a competitive advantage for the organisation. It is also a strategy for continuous innovation, adapting the organisation, its strategies, products and process to the changing needs of society. These innovations are then replicated by other players in the market, contributing to the engagement of more stakeholders in this journey.

5 Some dos and don'ts

Dos	Don´ts
Think big, start small, move fast. With sustainability it is important to take bold steps as the challenges are significant. Take things one step at a time and move quickly to remain ahead of competitors as they will catch on quickly.	Try to do everything at once. Sustainability is complex and will require a systems view to understand all the issues and begin to address them.
Lead from the top. Much of the success of Banco Real's integration of sustainable development into the organisation has come from visionary leadership at the top of the organisation.	Underestimate the need for gaining commitment by the leadership of the organisation. If senior leaders are not committed, it will be very difficult to make real progress in sustainable development.
Be bold and take risks even if the rest of the market isn't with you yet. When Banco Real introduced the social and environmental risk policy in 2001, the rest of the financial sector thought this was beyond the scope of a bank. Today, most banks in Brazil have implemented some form of social and environmental risk policy. It is important to challenge paradigms in order to shift the system.	Hide from the issues. If you think that the organisation holds responsibilities beyond traditional ones, put processes in place to address these.
Integrate social, economic and environmental dimensions into strategies, products, processes and policies of the organisation. It is important that sustainability is integrated into the core business to give credibility to the movement and demonstrate that the organisation is addressing the tough issues.	Focus only on programs that do not have a direct impact on the core business. It is much more difficult to focus on changing or integrating sustainability into the core business, but don't allow this to deter you.
Integrate sustainability into the strategic planning process and set up a governance model to manage the overall process of integrating sustainability.	Create parallel planning processes as this will always compete with the mainstream strategies and objectives of the organisation.

Dos	Don´ts
Engage stakeholders in the journey. By engaging with clients, employees, suppliers and the community, much can be learned that can be used to strengthen and enhance strategies, products and processes. Results in sustainability cannot be achieved alone. It requires partnerships and synergies with other stakeholders in society.	Try to do everything on your own. Resolving social and environmental issues is complex and requires the collaborative efforts of diverse stakeholders.
Invite in and debate dilemmas seeking opportunities for win-win solutions. It is important to be transparent and share dilemmas and difficulties. Through being open in this way, the organisation can work together with others to address tough issues.	Think the organisation knows all the answers. The journey will be more difficult if the tough issues are not addressed and they will surely surface again if not addressed.
Invest in the education and engagement of employees at all levels of the organisation from senior management to more junior employees. Sustainability is a topic that requires the personal engagement of staff. If employees don't understand the importance of sustainability and have not embodied the concept, it will be difficult for them to integrate it into their day-to-day interactions with clients and other stakeholders. Sustainable development is about changing the culture of an organisation, impacting and influencing employees and other stakeholders, one by one.	Simply communicate. Communication is important but more depth and engagement is required for employees to come on board. This process takes much longer but is much more transformative for the individual, the organisation and society.
Adapt your approach for different departments and business lines. Sustainability doesn't work with a one-size-fits-all approach. Each business line and support function has a unique contribution to the sustainability movement.	Take a one-size-fits-all approach. This will cause frustration on both sizes as the issues and roles of the different functions are so diverse.
Adapt and evolve with the changing needs of society. Sustainability requires a continual scanning of the external environment to understand the changing needs of and new developments in society. Management models and corporate strategies will need to continually evolve.	Remain stagnant. This will not enable your organisation to remain competitive and on top of the most relevant issues.

6 Future challenges

The challenges society faces with climate change, social inequality and natural resource degradation are immense. The private sector has a critical role to play in contributing to the reversal of these trends. The financial sector in particular can play a leading role in influencing other sectors to integrate social and environment dimensions into their businesses through the policies and practices that are put into place. As new forms of measuring success become more mainstream, existing models will need to adapt to this new reality. Organisations that are aware of the changing trends and needs of society and that are more flexible, will be much better able to adapt and will be more successful in this new landscape. Banco Real is committed to continuously contribute to the evolution of society by continuously adapting its strategies and models and innovate its products, services and processes.

Over the last eight years, Banco Real has gained significant experience in integrating sustainability into its business. In December 2007, in response to growing demand by clients, suppliers and opinion leaders, Banco Real launched the "Espaço Real de Práticas em Sustentabildade" or "Real Space for Sustainability Practices" to share the organisation's experience in integrating sustainability with clients, suppliers and the wider public. Through online courses and forums, and in-class training programs, the "Real Space for Sustainability Practices" aims to support clients and suppliers in integrating sustainability into their business and raise awareness among individuals and organisations to "shorten the distance towards a sustainable world". This is yet another step in Banco Real's sustainability journey. "Banco Real has passed the point of no return," Fabio Barbosa says, "There is no turning back and this drive will continue regardless of the actions of any individual. Every one of us can make a difference."

References

Sustainability Report 2002/2003 – ABN AMRO Real, Human and Economic Values, Together, São Paulo, September 2003

Sustainability Report 2003/2004 – ABN AMRO Real, Human and Economic Values, Together, São Paulo, May 2005

Sustainability Report 2005/2006 – ABN AMRO Real, A New Bank for a New Society, São Paulo, April 2007

Website

www.bancoreal.com.br/sustentabilidade

The Road Towards Excellence: Total Involvement in Quality

The case of Post Danmark

Anders Jeppesen

Abstract. In 1998 Post Danmark launched a massive change process based on the TQM philosophy. This entailed systematic measures to steer the organisation away from the traditional government service culture developing it towards a more modern and dynamic organisational culture. As a result of this change process Post Denmark won the Danish Quality Award in 2004 and was a finalist for the European Quality Award in 2006. This chapter describes the background for the process as well as its objectives, and it offers insight into some of the measures taken and examples of the results achieved.

Key words: Total Involvement in Quality, The EFQM Excellence model

1   Introduction

In 1998 Post Danmark launched a massive change process based on the TQM philosophy. This entailed systematic measures to steer the organisation away from the traditional government service culture developing it towards a more modern and dynamic organisational culture.

Through the 80s and the 90s Post Danmark saw immense and numerous changes – as did most companies. Post Danmark, however, went through some rough ground coordinating the transformation. Examples include rationalisation projects in the late 80s and early 90s, reconstructing the government postal service into Post Danmark in 1995 and the major changes in 1996-97 to the distribution system affecting 15,000 postmen.

At the same time Post Danmark was facing business challenges in terms of increased competition from electronic media and the prospect of by and by loosing what was left of the company's former monopoly. Management lacked the proverbial red thread which could lead the company in the right direction.

Internal deliberations in 1996-97 led to the acknowledgement that management needed improving. On the face of it business was ok – the bottom line showed handsome profits. However, management was aware of the fact that in the long term their way of running the organisation would fail to ensure black figures on the bottom line – although the period from 1988 to 1995 had indeed yielded positive financial results.

In 1997 a major strategy project, in which fundamental management principles were dealt with, led to the launch of a proper TQM process. Our aim was to have our organisational culture focus more on our customers and to involve our employees in boosting the internal efficiency in order to improve Post Danmark's competitive power. Strong competitive power is still our goal.

With the blessing of management and board of directors the framework for the company's TIQ (Total Involvement in Quality) process was formed. We knew that it would be a long and tough haul. This article describes the background for the process as well as its objectives, and it offers insight into some of the measures taken and examples of the results achieved.

2   Background of the company

The history of Post Danmark dates back to king Christian IV who on 24 December 1624 issued a "Royal Ordinance on Postmen", called the birth certificate of the Danish Post Office. Nine postal routes were established. The most important route was the one between Copenhagen and Hamburg where letters, parcels and goods were transported by carriage; postmen who went on foot and only carried letters served the other routes.

In Copenhagen, a postmaster was appointed to set up office at Børsen, the Exchange in Copenhagen, two hours each day and personally handle administrative as well as practical affairs, so there was a perfect good reason why it was laid down in the Ordinance that he must be a "sober-minded and diligent man". In provincial towns which the postmen passed through they took lodgings in an inn, for instance, and the landlord was to accept and distribute letters to addressees who lived in places not on the actual route.

One of the most important functions of the Post Office was the exchange of information, and this was not only limited to the distribution of newspapers. At the post offices, the locals met with travellers to hear news of the outside world. The newspapers were scrutinised and their contents discussed. Mail delivery in Copenhagen began in 1806. In 1861, there was local delivery in the 17 Danish towns which had more than 6,000 inhabitants and from 1865, the service was introduced in all towns. The rural routes were introduced in 1860.

On 26 October 1859, an ordinance was issued to the effect that houses in Copenhagen were to be provided with numbers! Kongens Nytorv (the then central square in Copenhagen) served as a starting point and houses on the right side of the street when walking away from Kongens Nytorv were given even numbers and houses on the left side of the street odd numbers. Until then, people had managed by saying/writing for example: "... in the fourth house after the golden lion when you go east". In 1967 postcodes were introduced as an element in the rationalisation of mail sorting.

Post Danmark provides basic postal services to all customers – senders as well as recipients – in Denmark. The aim is to have these postal services be the best in Europe, measured in terms of service level, quality and price combined.

Post Danmark is subject to a universal service obligation, which secures the whole population access to postal services on specified terms and conditions. Post Danmark has an exclusive right to distribute domestic letters weighing less than 50 grams.

In 1995, the mail delivery monopoly was broken, allowing more undertakings to distribute letters. Today, Post Danmark generates more than half of its annual turnover of approximately EUR 1.6 billion in competition with other undertakings.

In 2002, Post Danmark became a public limited company fully owned by the Danish State. In 2005 CVC Capital Partners bought 22 percent of the shares and the employees bought 3 percent of the shares in Post Danmark. In October 2005 Post Danmark and CVC Capital Partners became a minority shareholder in the Belgian Post, DePost-LaPoste. They bought 50 percent minus one share in the company.

With approximately 21,500 employees Post Danmark is one of the largest companies in Denmark.

3   What is TIQ?

In this section a general outline of Post Danmark's TIQ process is provided along with a description of the activities Post Danmark has launched and still uses as elements in TIQ.

3.1   Total involvement in quality

TIQ stands for Total Involvement in Quality. This is an accurate description of how Post Danmark perceives Total Quality Management as a concept. It's about quality in management, products, processes, partnerships and in our jobs – the word Total is to be taken literally.

From the very beginning our CEO took the lead in the TIQ process and was very careful in stressing that TIQ was a long-term process, **not** a project.

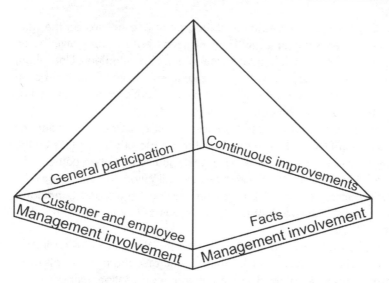

Figure 1. The quality pyramid

Table 1. Elements of the TIQ process

Management involvement	Focus on customers and employees	Continuous improvements	General participation	Focus on facts
Management development	Customer satisfaction analyses	Process orientation	Self-supporting teams	Customer satisfaction analyses
Education and training cascade	Employee satisfaction analyses	Lean	Employee satisfaction analyses	Employee satisfaction analyses
Rules of conduct	Process orientation	Total Productive Manufacturing (TPM)	Kaizen board	Process evaluations
Process orientation	Management development	Suggestion box	Kaizen	Goal monitoring
Goal monitoring	Self-supporting teams	Environmental system	Suggestion box	Benchmarking
Self-evaluation	The social chapter	Kaizen	TIQ training	Self-evaluation

The TIQ process is based on the following five basic elements:

1. Focus on customers and employees
2. Continuous improvements
3. General participation
4. Focus on facts
5. Management involvement

Management involvement is characterised as the core of the quality pyramid shown in figure 1 (Dahlgaard, Kristensen, & Kanji, 1998).

The TIQ process involves a large range of activities that are linked to one or more of the five basic elements of TIQ. Table 1 shows some of the activities Post Danmark has launched and still uses as elements in the continuous TIQ process.

The backbone of the TIQ process is the EFQM Excellence model which also forms the basis of The Danish Quality Award. The EFQM Excellence model is shown in figure 2.

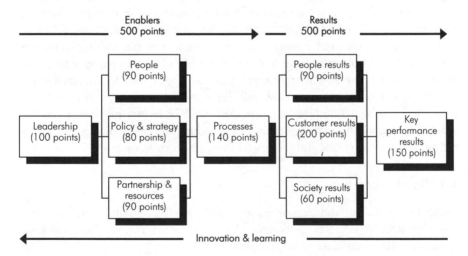

Figure 2. The EFQM Excellence model

In the following sections some of the crucial elements of TIQ will be described under the umbrella of the nine criteria from the EFQM Excellence model.

4 Leadership

In this section some of the crucial elements of TIQ related to the leadership criterion from the EFQM Excellence model are outlined.

4.1 Total commitment

From the very start Post Danmark decided that the TIQ process as such was to be supervised by top management. Of course, consultancies were brought in for sub-projects and still are, but not in any general way. This requires our total commitment and the integration of TIQ in our everyday routines. TIQ is not a buzzword management task but a question of another kind of management.

4.2 Education and training cascade

A good example of practical involvement was the education and training cascade, which marked the launch of TIQ. It started out at the management level and went on to comprise all employees. In the courses for level-1 bosses (e.g. regional managers) management was in charge of parts of the training. In the courses for level-2 bosses the regional manager would be in charge of some of the training, etc. The rest of the course was left to professional, external instructors. This system required bosses and managers to pay particular attention as they knew they would later have to transfer the gist of the course to their subordinates. At the same time it gave employees an opportunity to discuss the TIQ process with their managers. How will this course benefit me? How will TIQ affect me? It took 18 months from the start in 1998 before all permanent employees had gone through the course. The education and training cascade is the main reason why Post Danmark won the Danish HRM award in 1999.

4.3 Rules of conduct

Based on our values and mission as well as on the TQM philosophy, management formulated 10 rules of conduct for good leadership in Post Danmark. These 10 rules of conduct are shown in table 2.

The term "rules of conduct" may perhaps sound a bit compelling, but they are specific, measurable examples of desirable behaviour which overall cover the quality pyramid. The rules of conduct still apply to managers at all levels; they are a manifestation of what employees may expect from their managers. Post Danmark does an annual survey of whether bosses and managers abide by the rules of conduct – among other things through employee satisfaction analyses and through self-assessment. This brings the manager role and managers' behaviour very much out into the open.

Table 2. Rules of conduct

1. Management must be holistic to ensure sustainable results.
2. Goals and expectations must be based on facts and dialogue.
3. Displaying results is the platform for continuous improvements.
4. All units, teams and employees are aware of the importance that customers attach to quality.
5. Continuous improvements are only achieved by involving everybody.
6. Employees' knowledge and skills must be maintained and developed continuously.
7. Knowledge about best-practice must be shared with colleagues and units at all levels.
8. All employees are aware of their responsibilities to act in a manner that makes it easy to be a customer
9. All employees must be well informed about Post Danmark's situation.
10. Self-supporting teams are a central element in Post Danmark's organisation.

4.4 The Excellence model

The backbone of the TIQ process is the Excellence model. Annual self-assessments and assessments offer a systematic focus on continuous improvements in both "hard" and "soft" areas. Post Danmark sets great store by the Excellence model which helps us maintain an overall grip of the management of the organisation – at the company level as well as on the unit level. Since 1998 all levels have carried out self-assessment; subsequently internal assessor teams have visited units helping them to take an objective bird's eye. In the first trimester of 2006 all units thus went through their ninth self-assessment.

At the company level self-assessments were carried out by means of external, informal assessments in 2000 and 2001. In 2002 Post Danmark applied to the Danish Centre for Leadership for *Recognised for Excellence*, and in 2004 Post Danmark filed an application to the Danish Centre for Leadership for the Danish Quality Award. Early in the TIQ process management and all unit managers underwent assessor training with the purpose of getting a thorough understanding of the Excellence model. Furthermore Post Danmark has trained an active assessor team of app. 225 managers and specialists who undertake assessments in other units than their own.

5 Policy and strategy

This section outlines some of the crucial elements of TIQ related to the policy and strategy criterion from the EFQM Excellence model .

5.1   Europe's top postal service

Post Danmark's strategy builds on our mission identifying four focus areas which – via a number of projects and activities carried out in accordance with our values – will support the realisation of our vision. The strategy is illustrated in figure 3.

We have changed our strategy process from extensive analyses and strategy development activities every third year to an ongoing process involving an annual review.

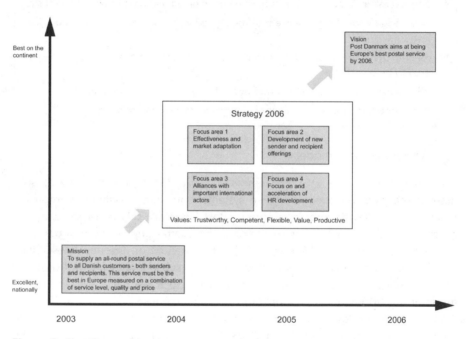

Figure 3. Post Danmark's strategy

Our ability to realize our vision of becoming the top postal service in Europe by 2006 is measured in two ways: partly through obtaining a place in the finals for the European Quality Award in 2006, partly through result benchmarking with the other important actors on the European postal market on a number of key figures covering customers, results, employees, society results and financial key results.

6   People

In this section some of the crucial elements of TIQ related to the EFQM Excellence model's people criterion are outlined.

6.1   Denmark's largest workplace introduces new work methods

Measured on number of employees Post Danmark is one of Denmark's largest companies. Irrespective of the increased automation of operations, the heart of the organisation now and in the future is our competent workforce.

Self-supporting teams

The launch of the TIQ process in 1998 was complemented with a long process of changing the work methods of our entire workforce. This was a consequence of having introduced self-supporting teams in production, distribution, at the post offices and in administration. It was a contest with many years of traditional role distribution of managers distributing and supervising tasks and employees merely following orders. The aim was to motivate employees to take on more responsibility in planning, effecting, evaluating and improving their routines.

From line manager to coach

For the teams it was somewhat of a revolution having to change their conduct – and this also went for the line managers. Before the functional managers were traditional line managers (who were supposed to know all the answers), now their role changed into that of a coach whose job it was to ask all the good questions. As a consequence quite a number of managers were replaced in the period from 1998 to 2002 and at the same time the total number of managers was reduced to half.

The first years were rather frustrating both for management and employees. Although the teams had been given a general framework within which they could organise their operations, there was no clear definition as to when a

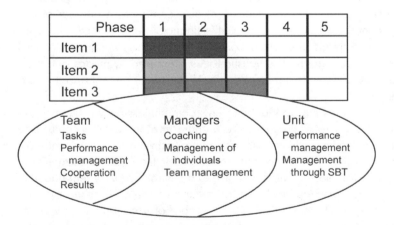

Figure 4. The SBT profile

team could actually be construed as being self-supporting. Not until the introduction of the Self-Supporting Team Profile in 2001 did it become concrete and measurable for the team, for the line manager and for the unit. The profile gave the teams guidelines as regards their tasks, goal-setting, and cooperation as well as how to evaluate their results. The SBT profile is shown in figure 4.

Each year there is a competition for the Self-Supporting Team Award which all teams can apply for. The application must contain a description of the team's work and their results. We have come to the point where Post Danmark can document a clear correlation between the development in the process of establishing the self-supporting teams and employee satisfaction.

6.2   The HR process

To aid staff management Post Danmark has a well-defined HR process with seven sub-processes ranging from recruitment and employment – over competence development – to the winding up of employment. All employees have a job profile that stipulates the offer of at least one employee performance review per year. At this interview the employee's professional and personal development is at the core, but the manager/coach may also focus on the organisation's values and attitudes.

7   Partnerships and resources

We apply a systematic approach to improving and extending our partnership relations which are important in the pursuit of our strategic objectives. The partnerships include five categories: commercial, supplier, social and sponsor partnerships as well as local partnerships. Our financial resources are handled in a holistic perspective. Earlier the business units were merely given guidelines for their financial targets, but now the target also comprises a number of parameters that contribute to creating the unit's financial performance. These include, among other things, the satisfaction of customers and employees as well as a number of process goals. The holistic focus is ensured by means of a hierarchy of goals that are jointly agreed upon between management and the self-supporting teams.

For a number of years the work put into environmental issues has been set up according to the ISO 14001 standard. We prepare environmental accounts and Post Danmark was the first within transport to compile an environmental status for our products according to international standards for life cycle assessments. In 2000-2001 all IT workplaces shifted platform to a central CITRIX system handling 7,000 users. The restructuring created a far better environment for the organisation to share its data; at the same time the number of user supporters was reduced by app. 70 percent. Since 2004 the development has been characterised by a sweeping SAP implementation and this will continue till 2007.

8   Processes

In this section some of the crucial elements of TIQ related to the process criterion from the EFQM Excellence model are outlined.

8.1   Key processes

Post Danmark has mapped its key processes. Management has specified the key processes that are critical in order to fulfil our strategy in accordance with our existing policies. Management's choices are based on the following criteria:

- Processes that are important to achieve our customers' satisfaction
- Processes that have a significant improvement potential

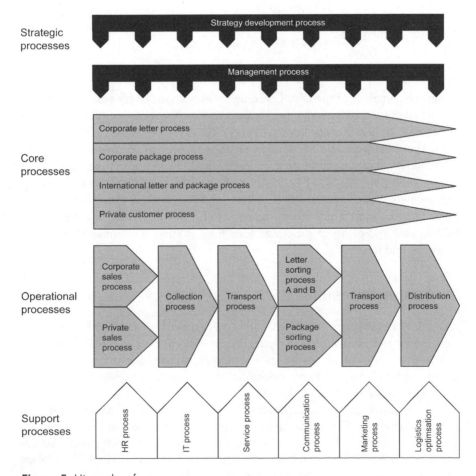

Figure 5. Hierarchy of processes

- Processes that are important to fulfil our strategy
- Processes that are of critical importance to the sustainability and results of our core processes
- Processes that are cross-functional, i.e. process activities are carried out in different departments/units.

This hierarchy of processes is illustrated in figure 5.

A deputy chief executive has been appointed to take charge of a particular key process. The process responsibility includes:

- ensuring a general mapping of the process;
- monitoring the process, including ensuring that the process cost level, time consumption and quality level are monitored and are improved; and
- initiating process improvements, including setting up process goals/improvement goals.

8.2 LEAN

The implementation of the LEAN production philosophy at all mail sorting centres, distribution centres and subsidiaries is among the most important elements in the effort to improve our core processes. Among other things LEAN includes value chain analyses, the elimination of non-value creating processes and the implementation of systematic process follow-up (bulletin board meetings).

Simultaneously the LEAN concepts of Kaizen (a culture that prescribes the improvement of work processes as a natural thing) and 5S (Sort, Set in order, Shine, Standardize, Sustain) are implemented. To a large degree measuring, guiding and improving of processes take their starting point in existing goals, measures and tools.

9 Customer results

In cooperation with the private consultancy Ennova Post Danmark has measured customer satisfaction and loyalty as an integral part of the TIQ process. With respect to external customers Post Danmark uses the international EPSI Rating model (European Performance Satisfaction Index) on which the Danish Customer Satisfaction Index is founded.

With the backing of the European Commission the EPSI Rating framework was developed in 1998. EPSI rating is a trademark of, and managed by, the European Foundation for Quality Management (EFQM), the European Organization for Quality (EOQ), and the academic network International Foundation for Customer Focus (IFCF) (Kristensen & Westlund, 2003).

The EPSI Rating framework is a structural equation model. The model stipulates that perceived value, customer satisfaction and customer loyalty are driven by company image, customer expectations, product quality and service quality. Each of these seven variables is seen as latent, i.e. non-observable, variables. Each of the latent variables is operationalised by a set of measurement variables. All questionnaire items have been evaluated by the customers on a 10-point rating scale that are subsequently rescaled to 0-100 to ease the interpretation of the results (Eskildsen, Kristensen, Juhl, & Østergaard, 2004).

The EPSI Rating framework is shown in Figure 6.

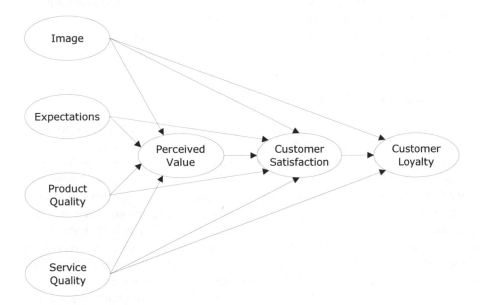

Figure 6. The EPSI rating framework

According to the EPSI model index 70-74 is equivalent to "good", and index 75-79 is equivalent to "very good".

In the time of the TIQ process Post Danmark has seen increasing satisfaction and loyalty from both our corporate and private customers (see table 3).

For internal customers Post Danmark uses an internet-based analysis tool. The internal customer/supplier relations have proved to be very important in expanding customer focus to all departments and all processes, but first and foremost because internal relations in an organisation of Post Danmark's size and structure is of great importance for the quality perceived by our external customers.

One of the indicators of customer satisfaction is that mail is delivered on time. On an average workday the number of domestic letters collected, trans-

Table 3. Customer satisfaction results

Private customers	1999	2000	2001	2002	2003	2004	2005	2006
Satisfaction	65	65	70	70	72	73	71	70
Loyalty	66	67	74	74	75	75	73	71

ported and distributed runs into approx. four million. This happens at a high level of quality compared to that of most other countries. According to IBM Consulting our precision rate was around 94 percent in both 2005 and 2006.

The letter handling quality in Europe and North America is measured on a regular basis by the International Postal Corporation. Here Post Danmark has been at the top for the past five years.

10 Employee results

The same trend of constantly increasing satisfaction is shown for Post Danmark's employees. Since 1998 Post Danmark has done an annual Job Quality Measurement. It includes 26,000 employees, 60 questions (1-5 scale) and it offers results at four levels: organisation, unit, workplace and team. A follow-up team level conference between coach and employees was specified as part of the process. At the conference areas of concern are determined, responsibilities distributed and goals are set for next year's results. This is laid down in the team's activity agreement for the coming year, which is checked every three months. In 2006 75 percent was satisfied or very satisfied (all in all) with their job situation. The response rate has been about 80 for the last four years.

One indicator that has been very important in Post Danmark after the restructuring of the distribution system in 1996-97 is the amount of overtime in distribution. Overtime fell from 4.5% in 1998 to 2.7% at the end of 2003. During the same period the number of workdays lost due to industrial action was reduced by a factor 19. Another indicator is a generally improved work climate between management and the workers' unions which in 2001 led to over 96 percent of all public servants accepting management's offer to work on a group contract basis.

11 Society results

Post Danmark has participated in AC Nielsen AIM's Corporate Image survey for several years. In the period from 1997 to 2003 the number of citizens who have a positive view of Post Danmark has increased from 51 percent to 67 percent which lately has placed Post Danmark in the most attractive quadrant in terms of knowledge vs. evaluation, i.e. among the "famous" companies with a high knowledge level and positive evaluation.

12 Key performance results

Over the last few years the net profit has been steadily improving. In 2006 Post Danmark, however, had the best result ever with a net profit of DKK 892 million. In the 2006 fiscal year the operating profit margin was 9%, return on equity was 34% and the solvency ratio was 36%. All in all the financial situation of the company has improved since the adoption of TIQ despite increasing competition.

12.1 The Danish Quality Award 2004

Among the key results Post Danmark also counts the self-assessment results according to the Excellence model. At the company level the feedback in 2000 from the external, informal assessors showed a score of 385 points. At the next assessment, which took place at the turn of 2001/2002, the external assessors' score was 467 points. After having applied for – and received – the Recognised for Excellence Award from the Danish Centre for Leadership in 2002, Post Danmark decided to apply for the Danish Quality Award in 2004. Post Danmark was given this award on a score which according to the Danish Centre for Leadership assessors was in the 550 to 600-point bracket.

The Quality Award was celebrated all over the organisation in various ways. Among these were 10 employee rallies across Denmark featuring some of Denmark's top performers. At these rallies the CEO thanked the Post Danmark employees for their excellent work.

In 2006 Post Denmark applied for the European Quality Award and received recognition as a finalist for this prestigious award.

13 The future

We have compared the extensive data material on customer and employee satisfaction with economic performance and have analysed the correlation between these in terms of our subsidiary network. The analyses show a clear correlation between satisfied employees to more satisfied and loyal customers to economic performance. The correlation is apparent but becomes even more unmistakable when parameters such as geography and customer volume are included in the analyses.

The results confirm our assumption from 1997. TQM and the Excellence model are not only a good idea. They are also sound business which later has been verified by Drs. Singhal and Hendricks (Hendricks & Singhal, 1997, 2001).

Many of the units' excellence scores will in the years to come reach a level where further improvement will become a challenge. Figure 7 shows the average excellence score for Post Danmark units since the launch of self-evaluation using the Excellence model in 2000 and until 2004 (1998 and 1999 saw stepwise implementation of selected criteria).

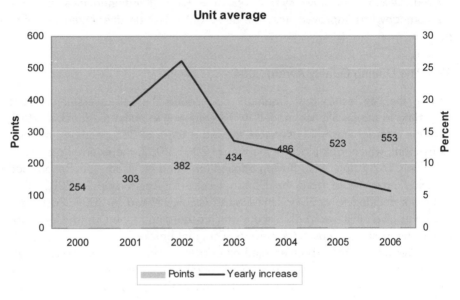

Figure 7. Average excellence score for Post Danmark units

Although it clearly is more motivating to strive for – and to reach – an annual increase of 50-60 points, fortunately the Excellence models can be adapted for consolidation at a stable high level.

The TIQ process has gone into its tenth year, but the process still has attention, backing and involvement from top management as at the launch in 1998. We are determined that Post Danmark would have been quite another organisation – and a lesser one too – if it had not been for the TIQ process. The agreement and accord in leadership that has led to progress in almost all areas is an important reason for the great interest in the organisation in connection with Ministry of Transport and Energy's upcoming sale of 25 percent of Post Danmark.

References

Dahlgaard, J.J., Kristensen, K., and G.K. Kanji (1998). *Fundamentals of Total Quality Management*. London: Chapman & Hall.

Eskildsen, J.K., Kristensen, K., Juhl, H.J., and P. Østergaard (2004). The Drivers of Customer Satisfaction & Loyalty. *Total Quality Management & Business Excellence, 15*(5&6), 859-868.

Hendricks, K.B. and V.R. Singhal (1997). Does Implementing an Effective TQM Programme Actually Improve Operating Performance? Empirical Evidence from Firms That Have Won Quality Awards. *Management Science, 43*(9), 1258-1274.

Hendricks, K.B. and V.R. Singhal (2001). The Long-Run Stock Price Performance of Firms with Effective TQM Programmes. *Management Science, 47*(3), 359-368.

Kristensen, K. and A.H. Westlund (2003). Valid and reliable measurements for sustainable non-financial reporting. *Total Quality Management, 14*(2), 161-170.

Principles-Based Governance of a Large Water Utility

Robert Humphries, Nicole Pettit, Natalie Reilly, William Varey, and Robert Kinnell

Abstract. The Water Corporation of Western Australia is a State Government-owned corporatised water utility which operates over the huge 2.5 million-square kilometre land area of Western Australia. The Corporation services a population of about 2 million people, has 2200 employees, an asset base of about AUD 18 billion, and an annual turnover of over AUD 1 billion.

The Water Corporation has embarked on a journey of business transformation, with environmental, social and financial sustainability as the prime conceptual and ethical drivers. This new focus on long-term sustainability has been catalysed by a dramatic decline in the yields of the surface and groundwater resources in the south west part of Western Australia – over 65% over the past 30 years, with demand growing at a rate of more than 3% per year.

The Executive of the Water Corporation has adopted 18 Business Principles as a thinking and governance framework, and these are being applied progressively.

Practical business benefits achieved so far include the Corporation's 'Security through Diversity' approach to sustaining water supplies in a drying climate; its commitment to achieve carbon neutrality by 2030; public targets for reductions in per capita domestic water use and wastewater reclamation; and the development of a multi-faceted biodiversity protection and enhancement program.

Key words: Water utility, Western Australia, drying climate, business principles, sustainability, business transformation

1 Introduction

The Water Corporation of Western Australia is a State Government-owned corporatised water utility, operating over the huge 2.5 million-square kilometre land area of Western Australia. The Water Corporation provides water supply, wastewater, and irrigation bulk water services throughout the State.

The business services a population of about 2 million people, has 2200 employees, an asset base of about AUD 18 billion, and has an annual turnover of over AUD 1 billion.

Over the past two years the Western Australian Water Corporation has taken steps to create a sustainable organisational culture. This is being approached by looking for ways to lessen adverse effects of the business on the environment, while doing so in socially acceptable and financially affordable ways.

The Corporation views the concept of sustainability as central to the way it does business and is implementing a comprehensive Sustainability Strategy which involves transforming key business processes. The Sustainability Strategy is being implemented through a structured change management process across the organisation. Fundamental to this change process has been the development and use of a set of 18 Business Principles.

This new business focus has already produced many positive environmental, social and economic benefits. These are discussed in this paper.

2   The business case for sustainability

The Water Corporation's commitment to systematically drive improved sustainability of its business was made in 2001.

This focus on long-term sustainability was catalysed by a dramatic decline in the yields of the surface and groundwater resources in the south west part of Western Australia – by about 66% over the past 30 years, with demand growing at a rate of more than 3% per year. The Corporation assumes that these declining water yields are driven by climate change (see figure 1).

The chronic nature of the decline in the availability of water from the environment was recognised in about 1996, at the time the Water Corporation was created. This realisation led to the development of a comprehensive strategic response – *Security through Diversity*. The *Security through Diversity* response to restore water security mimics the multiple pathways and diversity of natural ecosystems. It includes a range of responses – demand reduction, improved water use efficiency, new groundwater and surface water sources, water trading with irrigators, 'bio-engineering' forested catchments to increase runoff, water recycling and seawater desalination.

The sharp reduction in the availability of environmental water has resulted in accelerated capital expenditure of around AUD 1.3 billion in the Corporation's effort to re-establish the security of public water supplies in the southwest. The accelerated capital program has also significantly increased work pressures on staff.

Other challenges to the Corporation maintaining a 'business as usual' approach included:

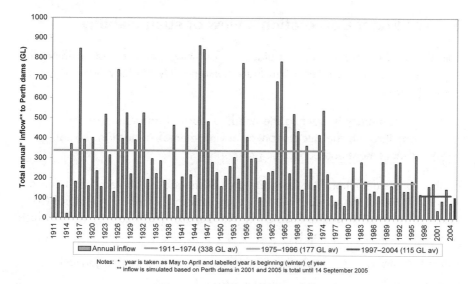

Notes: * year is taken as May to April and labelled year is beginning (winter) of year
** inflow is simulated based on Perth dams in 2001 and 2005 is total until 14 September 2005

Figure 1. Annual inflow to Perth's reservoirs, 1911-2005, showing that the current mean yield is 66% lower than the long-term mean

- a recognition of the finite capacity and the declining condition of Western Australia's environment

- increasing community concern over environmental issues, particularly global warming and climate change

- increasing diversity of social values around water

- industry reforms and increased regulation

- restrictions on budgets

- increased demands on employees

- changing community expectations regarding levels of service and consultation on business activities

- difficulties in recruiting and retaining talented staff during an economic boom.

During 2001 a series of scenario planning workshops involving external stakeholders and all senior managers across the organisation were run to address these strategic challenges and to generate responses to a range of possible future scenarios for Western Australia.

This resulted in a refocusing of the organisation's core business and recognition of the value of a triple bottom line approach to strategic business planning and performance reporting. This later evolved into a commitment to pursue an integrated approach to sustainability.

3   The Water Corporation's view of sustainability

The Water Corporation has adopted the following definition of sustainability outlined in the Western Australian State Sustainability Strategy – Hope for the Future (2003).

> "Sustainability is meeting the needs of current and future generations through the integration of environmental protection, social advancement and economic prosperity."

Further to this definition, the Corporation's Sustainability Strategy has been developed to reflect the concept of 'natural capitalism' described in Natural Capitalism – The Next Industrial Revolution (Hawken, Lovins & Lovins, 1999) which recognises four types of capital:

Human capital   – labour and intelligence, culture and organisation;

Financial capital   – cash, investments and money;

Manufactured capital – infrastructure, machines, tools and factories; and

Natural capital   – natural resources, living things and ecosystem services such as the production of oxygen by plants.

'Natural Capitalism' recognises and overtly values these four types of capital and acknowledges that for any activity to be truly sustainable in the long term, the overall value of all forms of capital must be enhanced and not degraded.

To continue in the long term, the business recognises that first three forms of capital above must not exist at the expense of natural capital, because society, the economy and the Water Corporation all depend on a healthy stock of natural capital for their continuing existence. Porritt's view of sustainable systems provides the conceptual framework for defining the Water Corporation's concept of sustainability (see Figure 2, adapted from Porritt (2005), p. 46).

The Corporation recognises that it must ethically play its part in systematically reducing, and then reversing, the harmful effects of its business on society and the environment. This means that to be truly sustainable in the long term, the business and the community it serves must operate within the limits imposed by the biosphere, and this means reducing its ecological footprint (see Rees, 1992; Wackernagel & Rees, 1996; Lenzen & Murray, 2003). It must also subject business decisions to a social benefit test, and attempt to mitigate harm if this occurs.

Emissions of greenhouse gases, particularly those derived from the consumption of electricity, comprise 70-80% of the Water Corporation's ecological footprint. To be true to its concept of sustainability, the Corporation has committed to operational carbon- or greenhouse gas neutrality by 2030. Another

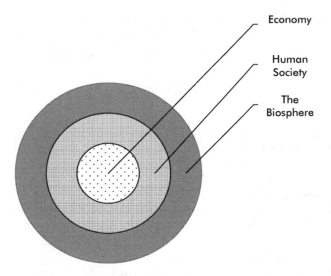

Figure 2. Sustainable systems

significant effect of the business is the permanent removal of biodiverse native vegetation for reservoirs, buildings and other facilities. Although this is sometimes unavoidable, the costs of compensating for clearing losses are usually small, and such compensation would be second nature for a truly sustainable company.

4 The Water Corporation's sustainability strategy

To enable the Corporation to undertake the fundamental shift towards an integrated approach to sustainability a comprehensive Sustainability Strategy was developed.

The five-year Sustainability Strategy has been endorsed, and is being progressively implemented by a small, dedicated team, which consults and brokers emerging opportunities throughout the utility. The Chief Operating Officer is accountable for the Sustainability program.

The strategy has been designed so that each individual, work team, business unit and operating division within the Corporation will engage in a process of becoming aware of, understanding, working with, and finally adopting the sustainability thinking and practices relevant to their role within the business.

The strategy supports the Corporation's Business Purpose:

> "The sustainable management of water services to make Western Australia a great place to live and invest."

The strategy is comprised of 17 programs which were developed to address gaps in the Corporation's capacity for sustainability. These gaps were identified from a review of the organisation's economic, social, environmental, political and governance capabilities.

Figure 3 provides an overview of the 17 programs comprising the Water Corporation's Sustainability Strategy.

1	**Best Practice in Water Management Solutions ♦** Design and implementation of new water management solutions to respond and adapt to climate change.
2	**Innovation Pilots for Win: Win: Win Outcomes ♦** Implementation of projects such as the Albany Environment Improvement Initiative, and the Shenton and Albany Sustainability parks that solve business issues in a significantly economically viable, environmentally and socially beneficial way.
3	**Lead Role in Local and State Sustainability Bodies •** Influencing agenda at a state level and national water level to raise the profile of water issues, climate change and climate adaptation.
4	**Key Stakeholder Relationship Management Program •** Development of structures and systems for improvements in stakeholder engagement generally, as well as at a business issue level (ie. Wastewater Management Framework) and project level (eg. South West Yarragadee Aquifer Project).
5	**Workforce for a Sustainable Future •** Recruitment, retention and development of people with relevance to the next 20 years of business needs.
6	**Community Education Partnerships ♦** Develop the delivery of Community Partnership Program.
7	**Sustainability Strategy – Implementation and Communication of Strategic Plan** Administration, implementation and communication support for the Water Corporation's Sustainability Strategy 2004/05 – 2006/07.
8	**Organisational Education and Awareness Program "From Principles to Action" •** Design, customisation, curriculum development and delivery of a sustainability education program for key sections leading sustainability within the Corporation.
9	**Sustainability Assessment for Integrated Resource Planning and Impact Assessment ♦** Integration of sustainability thinking and valuation into the Capital Process from Planning to decommissioning.
10	**Sustainability Regulators and Decision Makers Program •** Improvement of the regulatory interface by maturing the process for project sustainability with better outcomes in the areas of natural resources and environmental management.
11	**Sustainability Science and Policy Development •** Improvement in scientific knowledge in areas of sustainability and where current critical scientific uncertainty lies as well as development of compatible corporate policies.

Figure 3. Sustainability strategy 2005-2008

12	**Leadership in Social Sustainability Project ♦** Development of significant project(s) in the Socially Responsible dimension, which will solve a significant business issue or design a solution for a significant opportunity and demonstrate "Visible leadership in the community for Sustainability".
13	**Indigenous Cultural Strategy ♦** Coordination, management and development of an overarching Indigenous Engagement Strategy and identification of sub-projects. This strategy will build on, and show links between, priorities and strategies already in place or being developed.
14	**Building Sustainable Value •** Development of the approaches and techniques that will challenge conventional business paradigms and develop new thinking to drive the pursuit of sustainability throughout the Corporation and beyond.
15	**Marketing of Sustainability and the Outcomes •** Marketing internally and externally the brand, concepts of sustainability and the Corporation's actions of Sustainability.
16	**Sustainable Procurement – "Conscious Consumption" ♦** Improved approach to purchasing goods and services for the Corporation, incorporating sustainability assessment principles into the procurement process.
17	**Measuring, Benchmarking & Reporting Sustainability** Alignment of the Corporation's definition of success and definition of sustainability to what we measure and how we report our success. Participation in the Dow Jones Sustainability Benchmarking Index Survey.

Legend: • Making Better Decisions   ♦ Leadership in Sustainability

Figure 3 (continued)

5   Business principles

A key component of the implementation of the Sustainability Strategy was the development of a set of 18 guiding Business Principles (Figure 4). These principles were adopted by the Executive of the Water Corporation in 2006 as the thinking and governance framework for the business.

These principles are designed to support the implementation of the Sustainability Strategy by influencing thinking, policy, processes and activities throughout the organisation including:

- Executive decision-making
- Policy development
- Planning and evaluation
- Generation of options
- On-the-ground practices

- Engagement with the community and regulators
- Assessment of and discrimination amongst competing options

The business principles were developed after reviewing material from organisations providing world leadership in sustainability and consulting with the Water Corporation's Senior Executive. The draft principles were then tested for understanding and appropriateness with a diverse group of managers from across the organisation. They were further refined and then applied to past projects by technical staff to test them for applicability in a practical context by using them to assess how well prior projects were aligned.

Of the six dimensions of the Principles, the three outcome principle groups consider the social, environmental and economic effects of business decisions and actions. The three process principle groups (ethical, stakeholder and governance) describe the characteristics of a robust, inclusive, and conscious decision-making framework which will support sustainable outcomes.

Each principle reflects the Corporation's aspiration to prevent loss, sustain gains and enhance value across all of three outcome dimensions.

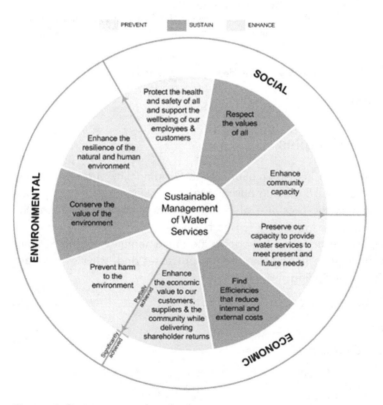

Figure 4. Business principles wheel

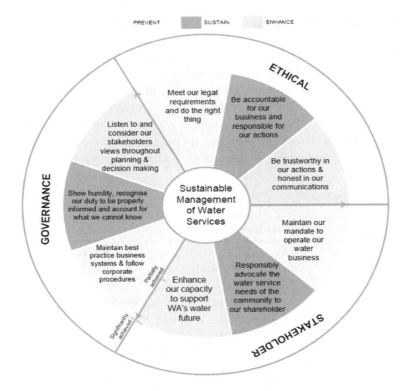

Figure 5. Business principles

6   Applying the business principles

The Business Principles are being progressively applied to the evaluation of options for executive and board decision-making, policy development and review, project planning and evaluation, on-the-ground practices, as well as community and regulator engagement.

The Business Principles are also beginning to be used to guide the design of processes, infrastructure, operations and interactions with others. In this context, they are used to frame, communicate and resolve the sustainability dilemmas of the business. Furthermore they are used to promote alignment of policies, processes and actions with the business purpose and the philosophy of sustainability.

The Corporation is also applying the Principles beyond its internal processes – to public engagement, to procurement and contracting, in the governance of alliances and in negotiations with community groups, government and key regulators.

7 Business benefits so far

The Water Corporation has already achieved significant business benefits from applying the approach to sustainability described in this paper. It is nationally recognised as Australia's leading water utility because of its successful adaptation to declining water availability. This contrasts with the situation of other major Australian water utilities, which are struggling to maintain water security and public confidence during the current period of severe drought in Australia. The table below summarises the major benefits realised so far.

Table 1. Business benefits from business principles

Action	Business Benefits
'Security through Diversity' approach to securing water supplies	<ul><li>Maintained community confidence & social 'licence to operate' for the business</li><li>Gained approval for greater capital borrowings to fund adaptation to the drying climate</li><li>Strong community support for the moderate water use restriction regime (>92% approval)</li><li>Avoided extreme water restrictions</li><li>Stimulated new avenues for business development – reclaimed water for industry; aquifer storage and recovery (ASR).</li><li>Improved business focus from publicly-stated targets for reductions in per capita domestic water use and water reclamation</li></ul>
Energy Management and Greenhouse Gas Abatement program	<ul><li>Much improved management of energy use, leading to better asset management and significant costs savings – ~AUD 1M/year</li><li>Achieved lower entry costs for renewable and low-carbon energy</li><li>Achieved synergies between disposal of wastewater to woodlots & carbon sequestration as offsets to GHG emissions</li><li>Gained national recognition by winning the Australian Greenhouse Office Gold Award in 2003</li><li>Gained community support, including willingness to pay for GHG abatement (Synovate Survey, October 2006)</li></ul>
Improving Decision-making in the Asset Planning & Asset Creation Process	<ul><li>Improved sequencing of planning process</li><li>Greater clarity of objectives; giving planners a conscious 'win-win-win' design brief</li></ul>

Table 1 (continued)

	• Lowest whole-of-life cost basis for choosing preferred asset development option (capital + operating) • More coherent & transparent evaluation of project options • Improved trust & credibility with community; more straightforward internal & external approval steps
Sustainability Awareness and Education Program	• Improved coherence & focus for the business • Greater engagement of staff with business direction; better alignment of personal & business values • Greater enthusiasm & innovation within the business • Cost savings & resource efficiencies from 'green office' programs • Achieved well-regarded community & business partnerships – e.g. Waterwise Schools program; improved governance of alliance contractors
Biodiversity Program	• Easier & less costly environmental approvals for capital works • Community support for conservation & habitat restoration via the Water Corporation's Cockatoo Care program • Restoration of biodiverse native vegetation via partnership with Men of the Trees Carbon Neutral Program

8   Conclusion

Whilst the process of embedding the Water Corporation's Business Principles is not yet complete, the application of this principles-based governance model is already stimulating excellent outcomes throughout the business, and the Water Corporation is becoming recognised as a national leader in sustainability throughout Australia.

The Corporation is taking an innovative approach which distinguishes it from many other organisation-wide sustainability initiatives. What is particularly distinctive is the preparedness of the Corporation's Board and Senior Executive to adopt a principles-based governance of the business in order to fundamentally transform it, and to integrate sustainability thinking and practice into the culture of the organisation.

References

Hawken, P., Lovins, A.B., and L.H. Lovins (1999). *Natural Capitalism – The Next Industrial Revolution*. Earthscan Publications Ltd, London.

Lenzen, M. and S.A. Murray (2003). *The Ecological Footprint – Issues and Trends*. ISA Research Paper 01-03.

Men of the Trees Carbon Neutral Program (see http://www.carbonneutral.com.au/).

Porritt, J. (2005). *Capitalism: as if the world matters*. Earthscan Publications Ltd, London.

Rees, W. (1992) Ecological footprints and appropriated carrying capacity: what urban economics leaves out. *Environment and Urbanization,* 4 (2) , 120-130..

Synovate (2006). Survey of Community Attitudes towards Greenhouse Gas Abatement for the Water Corporation.

Wackernagel, M. and W. Rees (1996). *Our Ecological Footprint: Reducing Human Impact on the Earth*. Gabriola Island, BC: New Society Publishers. ISBN 0-86571-312-X

Water Corporation (2003). Cockatoo Care Program. (See http://www.watercorporation.com.au/C/CockatooCare_index.cfm).

Creating Change by Delivering on Values

The case of Triodos Bank

Michel van Pijkeren and Peter Blom

Abstract. Triodos Bank was established to deliver social change by harnessing a commercial approach to its work. Driven by a vision to be a pioneer in sustainable development, the bank combines profitability and positive social and ecological impact. It has embraced a people-centred management model that emerged during a period of rapid growth over the last decade. This allows it to act as a bridge between value driven individuals and wider changes in society at large. This chapter outlines the emergence of a management model based on a blended value proposition.

Key words: value-based management, sustainable banking

1 Introduction

Although sustainability and triple bottom-line approaches have grown into widely recognised concepts across the business world, only relatively few enterprises start with a mission that is focused on contributing to society in a social, ecological and economic sense. Triodos Bank is an enterprise that is both value based and value driven throughout. As its name implies, the bank aims to create threefold value. And as a bank Triodos facilitates social renewal by making money available to individuals and organisations with distinct social, environmental or cultural objectives. It also aims to provide thought leadership creating space for sustainability initiatives to thrive, through lobbying, publishing articles and participating in external think-tanks and commissions.

Triodos Bank is built on human capital. It has a management model with people at its heart. It is a place where individuals connect and collaborate to get things done that they could not do alone. The results of this approach are clear. Its assets under management have grown strongly over the past 25 years. The services that the bank delivers have extended beyond taking savers' deposits and providing loans, into innovative funds and private banking.

2   Background of the company

2.1   Industry

The Triodos Foundation was founded in 1973 to finance projects and ventures that aim to deliver positive social change. In 1980, Triodos Bank was established in The Netherlands to foster social renewal, by using money in a conscious way. At the time this kind of change was typically a left-wing cause, pursued by non-governmental organisations and political parties. Businesses in general, and banks in particular, were part of the conservative establishment. The Dutch financial sector leaned heavily on 'Big Business' and was regarded as a pillar of the conservative establishment. The financial sectors' major interest was to finance the business community. Customers and society were less relevant and were paid only marginal attention.

But Dutch society was changing. In the sixties it experienced a feminist revolution and the rise of left-wing politics. The seventies were characterised by institutional change; working councils were established and a consultative governance model emerged in which the government, unions and business became institutionalised. In the eighties, however, an entrepreneurial spirit swept through the country; grass-root organisations championing social causes sprung up and new business ventures developed. Against a backdrop of a society in transition Triodos Bank established a business to live up to these new ideals. Now the bank employs 350 people, has almost EUR 3 billion in assets under management and made a profit of EUR 6.1 million in 2006. It has branches in Belgium, Spain, the UK and Germany and maintains numerous partnerships with financial institutions in the developing world.

2.2   Organisational identity

Triodos Bank exists to foster social renewal through innovation and entrepreneurship; as such it was established as a business instead of adopting a charitable or cooperative structure. As a business, Triodos Bank was free to renew itself and to establish innovative strategies without the potential restricting interests of a membership structure. It wanted to demonstrate that a business could reconcile profit and social development. It aimed to change the face of the Dutch banking industry through offering a values-based alternative to the mainstream. This is a people-centred approach, in the sense that it is not the product, the business plan, or the organisation that is central to the management model – it is the people behind and working with the organisation that count. Triodos Bank's mission reflects this focus:

- to help achieve a healthier society and enhance people's quality of life;

- to enable individuals, institutions and businesses to use money more consciously in ways that benefit people and the environment, and promote sustainable development;

- to offer customers sustainable financial products and high quality service.

This people-oriented approach also becomes apparent in Triodos Bank's business principles, which reflect the way the organisation operates. Triodos' identity develops through its co-workers' activities, the projects it cultivates and decisions it makes. The principles are formally laid down as the following:

- Transparency: Triodos Bank is transparent and open in the way it invests the money deposited and invested with it. Because money flows are increasingly complex and fast, Triodos Bank is transparent to customers and other stakeholders about its investments, profits and the causes it supports. To demonstrate this, Triodos Bank was the first bank to adopt the Global Reporting Initiative (GRI) sustainable reporting principles.

- Entrepreneurship: Triodos Bank supports initiatives that generate profit and social value. This requires commitment and responsibility from all its co-workers. In this context, every co-worker is an entrepreneur.

- Excellence: Triodos Bank strives to improve its processes and the way it works. It is a business that always seeks to develop its organisation.

- Sustainability: relates directly to the bank's mission to help facilitate social renewal. Triodos Bank aims to bridge the separate worlds of people, culture, nature and developing countries by financing sustainable initiatives and offering opinion leadership.

2.3 Product portfolio

To accomplish its mission, Triodos Bank supplies a specific set of financial services. It began as an intermediary between lenders and borrowers offering people who wanted their savings to be used ethically, the assurance that their money would only be lent in a sustainable and constructive way. And it continues, to this day, to lend only to companies that benefit people and the environment.

Triodos has the knowledge and experience to assess how to lend to businesses committed to creating sustainable value. It distinguishes itself from conventional banks by focusing primarily on what a business sets out to achieve, rather than its profitability. The first consideration is whether a venture is sustainable and fits with the bank's mission. Only after this is established is financial analysis undertaken. Besides conventional savings and loans, Triodos also offers investment funds and private banking services. During the last decade these services have increased in scope and now make up a significant part of the product portfolio.

2.4 Strategic direction

Triodos Bank has experienced significant growth since the late nineties. To make more of a positive impact and to further improve the quality of life where it operates, its strategy is to expand further. This strategic direction is based on three pillars:

1. Improving customer relations: Triodos Bank wants to support individuals who want to make a positive difference through conscious decision-making. It does so by making money available to an increasing number of customers. To increase its customer base and move closer to them, Triodos will increase the number of branches it has and countries it works in.

2. Triodos aims to develop a 'credible set of services', from its current limited base. In the future it will increase them, meeting most of its customers' financial needs. To be able to offer these services the bank will focus on product innovation. This will come from matching the ideas that spring from the bank's vision with customer requirements. These innovations should exceed the customers' needs; benefiting a wider range of stakeholders. These services will be distributed through diverse channels.

3. Finally, the bank is focused on 'Thought Leadership'. It participates in the public debate about social issues. It does this because it wants to be a force for social change and create fertile ground for its products.

The strategy seeks to manage the transition phase the bank is now in; from a small-scale mission driven bank to a professional, value driven organisation. The difficulty in doing it is to manage increased social impact, a larger customer base and an extended product portfolio, without losing sight of its mission. Triodos Bank is at the stage where it needs to integrate value based banking and customer service professionalism. The next section outlines the way Triodos uses a people-centred management model to achieve this.

Triodos Bank has developed its own identity over more than 25 years. Several events have had a critical influence on the emergence of the bank's distinctive identity and management model. The first was the founders' decision not to take a place on the Board, creating room for others to establish and drive the organisation. Following this example, Triodos Bank does not criticise the practices of others but demonstrates that a more sustainable approach is possible. In practise this means that Triodos Bank is not against banking and the mainstream banks, but just wants to do things differently.

The Chernobyl disaster in 1986 created awareness among the public at large of the critical role energy generation has on all our lives. It drew immediate attention to the way society was exploiting the Earth's natural resources. This situation offered Triodos Bank an excellent opportunity to position itself as working pro-actively to find solutions to these green issues.

A third event encouraged the bank to internationalise its scope and operations. Triodos Bank was asked to support local initiatives to help foster social development in several countries outside The Netherlands. From these contacts a network of interested parties was established, brought together by shared problems and an appetite for similar solutions. Through several collaborations the bank supported the development of microfinance in the eighties. This innovative tool enabled banks to empower people in developing countries on the basis of partnerships and equal business relations.

Triodos Bank's identity is characterised by entrepreneurship driving social renewal. To put its mission and values into practice, the organisation explores business opportunities that move beyond a narrow concept of a strictly financial value proposition. The bank recognises social issues and looks to find commercial solutions while being both profitable and financially sustainable. Reconciliation of profit and social renewal is possible because of a people-focused management model. The management model emerged through a process of practice and reflection. This process is always firmly grounded in the mission of the bank.

3   The management model in practice

The management model can be seen as the mental map providing an organisational context for the way people relate and operate within the organisation. The people make the organisation as much as the organisation gives people a platform for personal expression and development. The model shapes the context in which co-workers operate and develop, and outlines what is expected of them. Its goal is to create room for leveraging people's competences, to harmonise conflicting opinions and to drive forward organisational development.

The main building blocks are the roles co-workers take on. These roles resonate with the values underlying the organisation. Triodos Bank co-workers contribute to the organisation's mission in the following ways:

1. entrepreneurship

2. management

3. leadership

By relating these roles to organisational functionalities, the individual and the organisation mutually enhance one another, as in shown in figure 1.

1. The entrepreneur takes the initiative to develop business opportunities. He is innovative and takes responsibility to follow them up. The entrepreneur is the driving force that renews the organisation through product and process innovation, enabling the organisation to grasp new business opportunities. Through the introduction of new products and services, the bank is able to extend its scope and to increase its social impact.

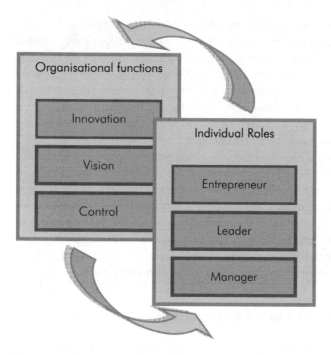

Figure 1. Connecting roles and functions

2. The manager assures the quality and improvement of operational processes. In striving for excellence, Triodos Bank seeks to continuously improve its products and processes. The manager safeguards the quality of performance, measuring, analysing and improving, in the pursuit of consistency and alignment. They are the stabilising force within the organisation.

3. The leader develops a holistic view of the organisation. They seek to integrate apparently conflicting roles of the entrepreneur and the manager. They set out the strategic direction and harmonise innovation and stability. They hold the Bank's vision and put the pieces together to create synergy and meaning.

In annual appraisals, expectations of roles and performance are discussed. Managers try to harmonise personal, career and organisational development. This stems from the conviction that the organisation has a bridging function between people and society at large. The organisation can ideally be the stage where people develop their competences in a way that adds value for wider society. The challenge is to find shared values between the individual, the organisation and society. These can be seen as three levels of development (See Figure 2):

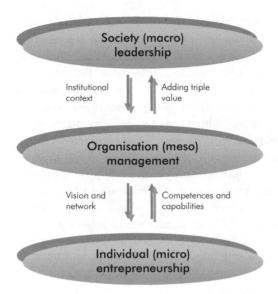

Figure 2. The bridging organisation

1. **Society:** Society is the highest aggregation level of development. Sustainability which preserves human development is a central governing principle. Society is the ultimate platform to set conditions for development. It is the stage where government, civil society and business interact to create institutions that promote human and organisational development and constrain opportunistic behaviour. The relationship with wider society requires strong leadership.

2. **Organisation:** The organisation offers a vision and platform to develop individuals' competences. It is the place where individuals can connect and collaborate, to create things that they could not do alone. These collaborative efforts are directed through the vision of an organisation creating value for society. The organisation should align its vision in order to create value that meets society's expectations. Strong management is needed to organise the tension between individual effort and macro developments.

3. **Individual:** The individual's abilities help to build the organisation. They are not only central to the organisation; through their actions the individual becomes the organisation. They collaborate with others developing themselves and creating a sense of meaning. They also contribute to the organisation's vision and strategy. Only through entrepreneurship can individuals play their unique role.

Although specific qualities are needed at different levels, the roles of the leader, the entrepreneur and the manager remain key. At every level there is a need for direction and integration. Without it society would fall into chaos, unable to foster collaboration and synergy, and ultimately to create value, the individual being lost without a sense of meaning and connection. At every level there is also a need for renewal and development. In its absence, society would lose the ability to create the institutional conditions needed for organisations to operate and prosper. Organisations would not match the competition or be able to attract and retain talented individuals. Without it individuals' competences would lose their value to the organisation. And at every level a stabilising force is needed. Otherwise society would drift, undermining the institutional stability needed for organisations and individuals to have a point of reference on which decisions can be based. Without stability the organisation would rush into new ventures without making the most of existing products and processes. Without stability the individual would lose a sense of identity and the time to reflect and learn.

Aligning the values and competences of the individual and the organisation forms the building blocks of society. It directs individual development in a way that creates added value for society. The organisation mediates between the established social institutions and individual aspirations. It is the management's task to organise this bridging role. This means managing an area of tension where conflicting interests and needs collide. For Triodos Bank this dynamic is not anchored in the present. It is about the tensions in The Netherlands, the European Union and developing countries, both now and in the future.

Triodos Bank seeks to balance the roles of leadership, entrepreneurship and management to have a positive impact on the individual and society at large. Managing this tension is not so much a matter of defining job profiles and assigning people to roles, nor is it just about measuring performance. This is not to say that these are inappropriate instruments, but that these instruments are not the key to human and organisational development. It is about connecting people to one another and aligning their visions for the future. It is about creating networks and awareness to identify and grasp opportunities. It is about finding a balance between the general and the specific, and between the whole and the parts. Individuals need to be able to make sense of their specific contribution to the whole organisation. It is the managers' task to create a space that enables the individual to get things done. Initiative, development and responsibility go hand in hand. Working in collaboration creates responsibility for colleagues, for suppliers, for customers and for other stakeholders.

As various management models have emerged Triodos has used several management instruments. They ensure that the bank's mission and values are translated into organisational action.

4   Deployment and experiences with the management model

The management model aims to find the right balance between the values of, and dynamic between, the individual and wider society. Triodos acts as a bridge in this process. And to establish this balance and meet the needs and expectations of individuals, organisation and society several management instruments have been deployed. They are established on both a macro and a micro level:

- At the macro level scenarios are created for possible future developments;
- At the micro level a horizontal process architecture has been implemented. This flexible matrix approach builds platforms where people can reconcile their individual aspirations with the global priorities of the organisation.

4.1   Scenarios and strategy

Triodos Bank is a credible force because it is committed to social renewal. As such it has to keep abreast of current and future developments within society. The bank uses scenario planning to help identify future trends and developments, guiding its strategic positioning. Thinking in this way creates awareness among co-workers about the context in which the bank and they themselves operate. Three high-level scenarios have been drawn up with this in mind:

1. *Holistic*: Society will develop robust links between economic, ecological and social life. This connectivity is based on a human perspective, which places human value and dignity at the heart of analysing problems and finding solutions.

   The bank's role in a holistic scenario will change significantly. Its banking services will become standard because of wide customer demand. Triodos Bank risks losing its strategic distinctiveness, as other banks innovate to supply the same set of services. To stay ahead Triodos Bank must deepen its range of services and develop new areas.

2. *Technological*: Problems are viewed from a technological perspective, using technological logic and instruments to shape society's growth. Triodos Bank will adopt a contrary, human voice. It will focus on opinion leadership and anticipate and drive through alternative solutions. The bank will be distinct as a niche player offering inclusive, human-orientated solutions.

3. *Disaster and depression*: In a society's worst-case scenario conflict between groups of people will increase; between poor and rich, informed

and ill-informed, dependent and independent. Environmental conditions deteriorate and social structures collapse. Contemporary institutions will not be able to deal with the threats inherent in this kind of profound change.

In this scenario Triodos Bank will adopt the role of a key enabler of grass root initiatives that meet people's fundamental needs.

These scenarios lead to questions such as: 'what kind of people do we need in which scenario?' and 'how do we design our organisation given a certain scenario?' They create the macro context in which the bank can consider strategic issues. What are society's needs and expectations given certain developments, and what does this mean for our products and services.

4.2 Process and structure

Triodos Bank uses a horizontal process structure to build an organisation that bridges individuals' aspirations and society's institutions. It aims to give co-workers full responsibility for the whole customer relationship process, fostering close relations between the two. This produces valuable information in turn, encouraging product and process innovations. In addition to their functional tasks co-workers can establish project teams to try and turn new ideas into new service concepts. A successful example is the Culture Fund, established in The Netherlands in 2006. Innovation synthesises new ideas, the organisation's vision and societal needs and expectations.

4.3 Roadblocks

As a socially responsible bank Triodos faces some unavoidable dilemmas. One derives from the need to value the positive sustainability content of a variety of ventures while, at the same time, ensuring that it is profitable and offers a reasonable return on investment. The bank continuously has to reconcile these values. It has built a great deal of experience in assessing these issues, but in the face of its current growth, numbers have become increasingly important. An example is the proposed increase in the bank's operating result from an historic level set at 4% to 7%. Several shareholders have expressed their concern about increased dividend rates, for fear that they will keep the bank from fulfilling its social mission.

Triodos Bank's visionary ambition also depends on co-workers who have their own aspirations, competences and limitations. For an organisation with a people-centred management model, the people it employs and their capacity to deliver are the starting point of assessing what is possible. The management challenge is to align the organisation's development with the biographies of its co-workers.

4.4 Results

Because it adopts an unconventional management model, detailing its results is difficult. Nevertheless, this section describes some internal and external impacts delivered through its deliberate vision and operations.

4.5 Economic value

Historically, Triodos Bank aimed to achieve a 4-% annual profit. Recently this increased to 7%. From 1999-2004 the bank's profit was on target. But its profitability is lower than that of its competitors because of extensive investment in growth and the development of new markets. Ultimately, the bank's main objective is not to maximise its profit but to make as much social, environmental and cultural impact as it can, and to do this in a sufficiently profitable way as to ensure its ongoing development. Alongside increases in profitability Triodos Bank has experienced extraordinary growth elsewhere over the last five years:

Table 1. Growth figures of Triodos Bank (Triodos Bank, annual report 2006)

	2002	2003	2004	2005	2006
Total income *	22.6	24.9	30.2	36.6	45.9
Net profit *	2.6	3.0	3.6	5.3	6.1
Total assets under management per co-worker *	6.2	6.8	6.9	8.0	8.5
Total assets under management *	1.282	1.526	1.818	2.406	2.958
No. co-workers	206	224	264	301	349

* amounts in EUR millions

4.6 Social innovation and impact

Triodos Bank makes a considerable impact by lending directly to responsible business initiatives. The bank's lending is in the following areas:

1. Nature and environment: this sector covers projects such as renewable energy, solar and wind energy, organic food and agriculture and environmental technology;

2. Social business: this sector includes projects and ventures with clear social as well as economic objectives. Examples are businesses that preserve tradi-

	tional skills and advisory and accounting support for start-up enterprises;
3. Culture and welfare	in this sector loans are made to organisations active in education, health care and support for individual artists;
4. North-South	microfinance institutions are supported in developing countries and loans are made to fair trade initiatives in this sector.

Triodos Bank offers financial services and creates opportunities for businesses and charities working in clearly defined areas. By lending to, and empowering these organisations, they become more professional and create social as well as economic value. In this way Triodos Bank impacts society in a much broader way than its immediate operations. It not only drives product innovation, such as microfinance and green funds, but social innovation by financing innovative, value driven ventures.

4.7 Sector impact

Over 25 years Triodos Bank has pioneered new investment areas. Through its sustainability approach it has opened up sectors, such as the arts and culture, small-scale wind energy projects and the organic industry, to lending and investment. While conventional banks ignored these areas, Triodos recognised the positive social impact they could make and assessed whether it would be financially viable to invest in them. It has highlighted the importance of these industries for other banks which are now following Triodos into them. As a result ventures that once relied on government subsidies, can now attract capital and become independent successes.

5   The future challenges and how the model will be adapted to meet them

Triodos Bank faces a number of short-term challenges, which can be defined by the following scenarios:

- The efficiency and quality of processes becomes increasingly important. To innovate and develop close relationships with your customers means smooth, tightly controlled processes. Triodos wants to combine its pioneering role in sustainable banking with excellence in developing and supplying quality processes.

- Because Triodos Bank is a business with a value driven mission it aims to increase its social impact by expanding its customer base. This means numbers are important. But they must not prevail over the values and the mission of being a sustainability pioneer. The dilemma is then to increase the bank's size while maintaining and deepening its values and mission. Given its role as a bridge between the individual and wider society Triodos tries to harmonize the dynamics and values between the two. Within a growing organisation, where numbers become an increasingly important indicator of success, management aims to secure space for project teams to cultivate new ideas. In this way the organisation tries to reconcile the need for control with its pioneering vision. Through its close relations with customers and social institutions Triodos anticipates future developments and translates them into groundbreaking products. But it can only remain a successful, inclusive institution through innovation and a high quality, efficient approach to everything it does.

Reference

Triodos Bank (2006) Annual Report 2005, Zeist

Website

www.triodos.com

How to Combine Managerial Performance with Social Responsibility in a Global Firm

The case of Gaz du France

Vincent Dufour

Abstract. This chapter raises the issue of the transferability of management methods as and when a company becomes more global. Although globalisation increases the potential for transferring standard management methods inside large international companies, it also increases the significance of cultural variables in behaviours and practices. This factor puts into question the widespread use of such management methods and raises new challenges for managers.

The effects of rapid internationalisation and the diversification of its activities have meant that Gaz de France has had to address these issues and adapt its managerial practices to its new context. The system it has developed to meet these new requirements seeks to combine respect for diversity with the need for coordination over the company's new scope of activity. It does not impose a single management method but rather proposes common references within which each manager is encouraged to continuously improve his or her practices, thus contributing to the group's sustainable performance.

Key words: Performance, sustainable development, human capital, socially responsible management, diversity, reengineering, best practices

1 Introduction

What is management? When managers are asked about their own management style or practice, they generally tend not to see it as a science, but prefer to define it as a personal aptitude or even an art by which they help people working under them to move in the direction desired by the company. This means that management practices are the result of cultural representations and constructions that reflect the values, standards, beliefs and priorities of a given point in time.

However, from the moment that the company expands outside its usual boundaries, it has to address different practices and representations, and it becomes more complicated to maintain the coherence of the new structure. Management methods previously operative may no longer be adequate, or may be misunderstood and even rejected by those to whom they are now proposed. Similarly, the limits of tools developed in the previous context may become apparent, and it may prove difficult to transpose the management method used hitherto unless a special effort to adapt it is made.

It is this effort to adapt that Gaz de France has made recently, and that this chapter intends to describe.

In recent years, Gaz de France has become a leading energy and services group, with strong international presence. As a result, it has had to re-examine its management method and has come up with an original solution which factors in the diversity of its components and facilitates the improvement of managerial practices, regardless of the manager's home country or culture.

2   From a national company to a leading European energy and services group

Established after World War II as an *Etablissement Public Industriel et Commercial* or *EPIC* (industrial and commercial public institution) under the French Nationalisation Act of 8 April 1946, the company's historic mission was to manage all gas industry companies in France. In the reconstruction context of that time, nationalising the gas industry appeared to be a necessity, given that a large number of facilities had become obsolete and were scattered across the country. The company was involved in the national rationalisation of investment in the gas sector and in the following years continued to work in the national interest by developing its gas transport and distribution activities across France.

Step by step, it built up its positions upstream and downstream in the gas chain, as well as in energy-related services, initially in France and then, from the nineties, in Europe generally. From this point onwards, market liberalisation gradually opened up the French market to competition, and in so doing, modified the rules of the game. This change – which will end with the full opening-up of the French market in July 2007 – has led the company to re-examine its *business model* and move beyond its traditional boundaries, embracing new opportunities in France and in other countries.

Doing so, Gaz de France has developed over the last ten years into a European-wide multi-energy and multi-service operator. Today, it helps to secure the continent's supplies and is in a key position on the market as one of Europe's main gas suppliers, serving almost 14 million customers and monitoring Europe's largest gas transport and distribution network. Second leading operator in gas storage and LNG terminals, it can rely on a diversified supply portfolio via numerous long-term contracts (Norway, Algeria, the North Sea, etc.) and a fast-developing exploration-production activity.

Gaz de France moved from a public to a private company in 2004. In July 2005, its share capital was opened, making the new "Gaz de France SA" one of Europe's main energy listed companies.

Number of employees	50,244
Turnover	€ 27.6 billion
Percentage of turnover abroad	40%
Percentage of workforce abroad	32%

Figure 1. Gaz de France group scope of activity in 2006

3   From a normative management model to an upgradeable management method

In recent years, the company's growth policy has had a direct impact on the company's traditional management model.

As the group opened up to the competition on its historic market and its activity began to extend beyond France, taking on board new businesses and new cultures, it had to investigate the best way of **managing diversity** and promulgating a new **performance culture** shared by all its components. Traditionally attached to social dialogue, and enjoying very strong local presence, it tackled this change by seeking the most appropriate management model in accordance with its new business strategy.

3.1   The old model

The work of the company's managers was originally aimed at a community of employees who all shared a strong feeling of belonging and the same professional culture, summarized in the generic term used to designate them as "gas workers". They belonged to a different community than did "electricians", doing often physical work, trained in the same schools and in direct contact with their elders, working close to ground level. They developed specific and pragmatic habits and behaviour, stood by each other and were strongly attached to the public service culture. Back then, the most widespread management method in the company was very typical of network industries and infrastructures, with hierarchical behaviours strongly geared towards the management of technical and industrial risks on the one hand, and on the other, regular contact between management and the trade unions both at the national and local levels. This type of **predominantly technical and social management** was a means of containing conflicts and maintaining proper control over technical risks, while at the same time investing in the development of networks across the country.

From the mid-eighties, things started to change. An alternative management method gradually began to assert itself alongside the prevailing one, albeit without taking its place. **The customer-oriented culture** spread widely to Gaz de France managers, linked with the development of a customer portfolio that has gone on growing ever since. These two management methods continued to co-exist in the years that followed.

The first signs of a merger between these two management methods came with the spread of **quality management** during the late nineties. The management by objectives and the introduction of quality processes enabled uniform performance standards to be disseminated throughout the group's units in France. This effort to standardize and align practices was also reflected in the training managers received in how to carry through annual appraisals for instance, and in the dissemination of a **Manager's Charter** from 2001. This charter recommended a set of managerial practices to be implemented, such as the use of formal annual appraisals, which became a widely-used tool for managing individual performance group wide in France.

3.2   The need for a change of model

Among the factors leading to the global transformation of the group's strategy, positioning, communication, management and culture were the opening-up of Europe's energy markets, the end of its monopoly and the loss of its Public and Industrial Institution status.

The opening-up of European markets to competition and Gaz de France's access to new markets via the takeover of other European gas and services companies resulted in a **reconfiguration of the group's staff**, who was used to different management methods and cultures. Although just a few years before regular meetings could be held with the company's managers – mostly located in France and sharing the same professional culture – from this point in time things began to change: the number of managers increased, they were spread out over different countries and their jobs were more diverse than in the past.

At the same time, the group's listing on the stock exchange in Paris exposed it for the first time to the **outside eyes of social rating organisations**, keeping a close watch on initiatives and practices in the human resources and social fields.

Lastly, the **group's medium-term growth policy** inevitably meant that it had to update its human resource management practices. It needed to integrate the new diversity appearing in its human capital and to make sure that it could become a source of competitive advantage to face future business challenges.

3.3 The choice of a socially responsible model appropriate to the company's new context

Thus, Gaz de France was prompted to rethink its management practices and make allowances for the more complex, more multi-cultural and less predictable environment in which it now found itself.

The *reengineering* of the group's management model was launched as part of its Industrial and Social Project at the end of 2003. At this stage, General Management defined a clear Human Resources ambition, socially responsible and expecting future employees to be:

- "Motivated, skilled and efficient"
- "Ready for changes in their jobs"
- "Loyal to their group"
- "Sharing and respecting common reference values."

To initiate this *reengineering* process, a project known as the "SRM project" (Socially Responsible Management project) and led by Corporate Human Resources Management was set up. Its objective was to establish **a set of management practice guidelines** which could be **applied group-wide** and that was **in keeping with its ethical commitments,** newly-defined at this very moment. These commitments to a large extent echoed the principles championed by social rating organisations, such as the fight against discrimination, equal opportunities, the value of social dialogue, health and safety or training and individual development.

In opting to take a fresh look at its managerial practices and taking up a position as a **socially responsible group**, the company demonstrated both its attachment to values firmly rooted in its culture (such as social dialogue, local proximity, solidarity, safety and the integrity of individuals) and its desire to accept the consequences of the increase in its scope of activity, taking advantage of its new diversity.

To take stock of this new scope, **a multicultural working group** representing the group's French and foreign subsidiaries (COFATHEC Services, ESS/Britain, PRONED/Holland, PREUSSAG/Germany, EGAZ-DEGAZ/Hungary) and parent company entities, was formed. It was tasked with two objectives:

- To conduct a comparative analysis of internal managerial practices,

- On the basis of that analysis, to come up with proposals for the establishment of new managerial guidelines.

The analysis revealed base practices that were up to the standard of international requirements (ILO), European standards, national laws and company internal regulations. Nevertheless, it brought to light a highly contrasting situation, characterised by **huge variations in practices** (from one business to another and/or from one country to another), that were inseparable from their economic, social and cultural context.

This observation had a direct impact on the proposals put forward, prompting the group to move towards **improving practices,** rather than towards a *top-down* kind of upgrade. At the time of this study, it emerged that even though a need for shared values was being felt, the group's new management guidelines could not impose a single standard, at the risk of producing the opposite effect to the one expected. The risk of stirring up rejection of what might be seen as an "imported" product, created *ex-nihilo* by the parent company, and therefore to a large extent "foreign" to local management, was clearly identified by the working group as one of the pitfalls that had to be avoided.

Consequently, the working group's recommendations related to two aspects:

- Firstly, given the importance of cultural context, practices were not easily comparable; it was impossible to extract any correct meaning from their comparison. It followed that **choices concerning improvements had to be made locally**.

- Secondly, because of the diversity of practices within the group, no shared HR and social ambition appeared. A **corporate system giving overall meaning was therefore needed**.

4   "PROMAP" good practice guidelines to help improve the performance of the group's managers

The "PROMAP" (PR.ogress in MA.nagement P.ractices) system was constructed on the basis of the mentioned "SRM project" recommendations.

4.1   The method used to construct the system

The method used involved two phases.

To begin with, a process to **identify best management practices** in effect in the company was embarked upon in 2005. A second working group was formed for this purpose. Using a questionnaire compiled by this working group and visits to the group's subsidiaries, a set of best practices emerged from the company as a whole. These reference practices were then grouped together in a summary document that could be sent out to every manager in the group. This document was divided into the following six chapters, each associated with the relevant reference practices:

1. Communicate with employees and staff representatives
2. Promote diversity and take action against all kinds of discrimination
3. Develop employability
4. Recognize and reward responsibilities and contribution in employment
5. Continuously improve working conditions
6. Anticipate and accompany restructuring

Secondly, if these guidelines were to produce the intended improvement in practices, they needed to be backed up by a **specific and more voluntaristic system** defined at the corporate level. The PROMAP system was developed to meet this requirement.

4.2   Decentralised implementation

The PROMAP system is used in a decentralised manner by local management. The system does not impose a standard management model, but rather aims to place each manager within his own usual professional environment, and make him aware of his responsibilities as regards the performance expected within that space. It does not provide any ready-made solutions, but instead expects the manager to improve his managerial practices by making appropriate choices related to his own local context, whence its name, „ PROMAP = PR.ogress in MA.nagement Practices".

To achieve this objective, local managers are invited by the senior management of their unit to:

1. Define their managerial priorities at the beginning of each year, using the group's reference practices as their basis,
2. Put forward annual objectives and the related performance indicators,
3. Feed back all of this information (practices used, objectives, level of achievement measured by indicators, and any singular points) to the senior management of their entities and to their HR department, so that data can be consolidated at the group level at the end of the year.

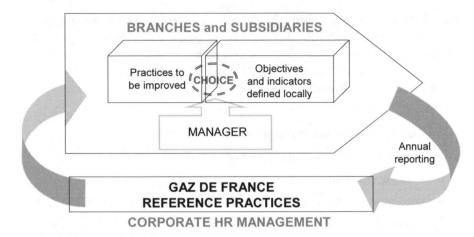

Figure 2. Decentralised implementation of PROMAP

4.3   The corporate level ensures coherence

The group-wide coherence of the Promap system is ensured both upstream and downstream.

Upstream, the reference practices are part of a **common base specific to Gaz de France**, compiled and sent out by the corporate level. The corporate level also steers the implementation of the system, which follows an annual cycle.

Downstream, the manager has to indicate the level of improvement he has reached in comparison with his objectives. **Quantitative and qualitative reporting** with respect to this improvement is incorporated into the group's social reporting, which is managed by corporate HR Management.

An **annual study of changes in the group's managerial practices** is produced at the end of each fiscal year to provide feedback and establish an improvement loop. This study is carried out on the basis of the quantitative and

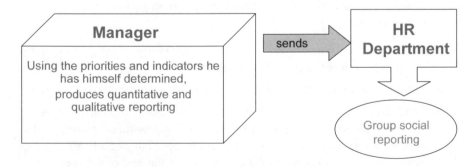

Figure 3. The annual reporting process

qualitative reporting, and highlights any innovative practices managers may have implemented during the past year. Where applicable, any such practices may be incorporated into the group's reference practices and be disseminated as such to all of the group's managers to provide input for their future management choices.

5   Pilot operation and widespread use of the system

Given the fact that this was a completely new system, it was decided to complete a pilot rollout in a subsidiary with European scope before bringing it into widespread use. In 2006, the pilot operation was conducted at COFATHEC, an energy services company which is part of Gaz de France's Services Business branch, employs almost 12,000 people and has five subsidiaries in France and three in other European countries (Benelux, UK, Italy).

No difficulties were encountered during the pilot operation, which identified four key factors for the success of the group-wide rollout of the system:

1. Subsidiary appropriation and empowerment driven by top management

2. The designation of PROMAP advisors at branch and subsidiary levels, responsible for powering the system

3. Clearly identified improvement priorities (progress plans) at each level (branch and subsidiaries), set out in managers' management contracts

4. Feedback steered at the branch level.

This pilot operation also enabled PROMAP's advantages to be assessed in comparison with the management method(s) in effect up until then:

- A transparent approach, easy for local management to adopt, and leaving plenty of room for subsidiarity,

- A limited number of priorities selected within a common reference framework, thus confining the number and dissipation of managerial messages,

- Managers who act as relays for the group's performance, because they are motivated to reach the objectives they have set themselves,

- Managerial priorities in keeping with the challenges facing the company and its development plan.

In the light of the success of the pilot operation, the rollout of the PROMAP system was extended group-wide during the first half of 2007, and its first reporting results are expected for the end of 2007.

5.1 PROMAP is … but isn't …

Table 1. What PROMAP is and what not

PROMAP is…	But isn't…
The improvement of managerial practices	An exhaustive table of indicators
A driving force behind good practices and optimisation of their use	A management toolbox
Local choices (subsidiaries) with respect to managerial priorities	Standard indicators
Benchmark practices that demonstrate the Group's ambition	A wide range of practices with no shared meaning
The commitment of all involved parties	"Just another HR thing"
Managers take action	HR does it for them

Ultimately, the system's success depends on the commitment of local level managers („micro"), within a global reference framework („macro") consisting of good practices previously selected within the group and whose implementation is checked at regular intervals.

6 Conclusion

In recent years, the path Gaz de France has experienced can be summarized as follows:

- first, taking a critical look at its management model with a view to adapting it to its new environment;
- second, developing a new model and adopting new references with the potential to ensure the group's sustainable ambition;
- third, spreading this model throughout the company.

Such a process is never an easy thing to go through. It came at a critical point in the company's history, when the pressure caused by the end of the gas monopoly, the opening-up of the market to competition and the conquest of new markets was dramatically increasing. It required substantial investment, and was very time-consuming, mobilising large numbers of people inside the company, both in France and abroad. In developing and implementing PROMAP, the company felt that when it came to management, „too many standards spoil the broth". The company chose to increase its responsiveness and competitiveness by accepting diversity in the behaviours and practices that make it up and considering them as an additional asset.

The contribution made by this diversity should enable the group's culture to evolve and keep pace with its new development.

References

Mendez, A. (2006). Vers une globalisation de la gestion des resources humaines. *La gestion des ressources humaines*, Paris, Cahiers français pp. 38-43

Whitley, R. (1992). Societies, Firms and Markets: the Social Structuring of Business Systems. *European Business Systems*, London, Sage.

Hofstede, G. (1994). *Living in a multicultural world*, Paris, Editions de l'organisation.

Hope Hailey, V. (1999). *Strategic Human Resource Management*, New York, Oxford University Press.

Website

http //gazdefrance.com

Competitiveness Through Co-determination

The case of Vandemoortele

Birgit Benkhoff and Helmut Lutzmann

Abstract. A margarine company in East Germany demonstrates that its cost minimization strategy in a highly competitive market can best be pursued not by moving to Poland or the Czech Republic where wages are only a fraction of German standards but by valuing its workforce. A coherent set of policies including good wages, multiple skilling, participation and emphasis on health and safety have created the trust that makes co-determination by the works council particularly beneficial. Generosity, openness and consistency on the part of management caused a sense of common purpose among employees who in turn contribute to a continuous downward spiral of costs. They created the most efficient production system in the industry.

Key words: Conflicts of interest, co-determination, integration, involvement, efficiency

1 Introduction

The German model of Industrial Relations, characterized by co-determination, is increasingly under attack. In times of deregulation and enhanced competition many employers regard it as restrictive, time consuming and costly (e.g. Wenger, 1986). The erosion of the system is particularly obvious in East Germany where unionisation is lower than anywhere in Germany. Only 20% of firms are covered by collective bargaining with trade unions and employee representation through works councils at plant level is restricted to 30% of enterprises.

Vandemoortele Deutschland has demonstrated that the German system of resolving conflicts of interest through employee participation has not only served the country well during the period of post-war economic growth but also provides the ideal framework for a management model designed to minimize costs and resist fierce competition. Based on traditional-style co-determination, the East German plant of margarine manufacturer Vandemoortele has become the paragon of cost competitiveness within the industry.

2   The company and its strategy

Vandemoortele Deutschland GmbH is part of a Europe-wide food manufacturing group. Its products (margarine, bakery products, soy products) have nothing that would make them inimitable. The company supplies mainly German food retail chains which are dominated by discounters. This market is characterised by low profit margins. Its suppliers are put under the same competitive pressures. Demand for products fluctuates considerably. Retail chains tend to place high volume orders. When another supplier offers a lower price, they take their business elsewhere. Their cancellations have a large impact on the producer. In this world of cut-throat food production the keys to competitiveness are low costs and reliable quality.

Vandemoortele, a family-owned limited company, started off with one production site in Belgium and is now the second largest margarine producer in Europe. The strategy was to increase its market share and become a player across Europe. Over the years Vandemoortele acquired factories in Spain, France, Italy and Germany. The plant in Dresden used to be one of the major margarine production sites in the former GDR; it was bought after the reunification together with two other German factories elsewhere in the country.

The value of the Dresden plant lay as much in the estate as in the excellent trade connections to Russia that came with it. The factory is close to the borders with Poland and the Czech Republic that import a large proportion of the produce. Apart from Russia, which until 1998 placed high volume orders, Hungary and Romania are also major customers.

With plants distributed across Europe, Vandemoortele is not very vulnerable to the impact of transportation costs. Its strategy is based on the expectation that petrol prices will increase over the years and that its network of sites will allow relatively short distances to the consumers and inexpensive transport.

Vandemoortele's competitors are set up more centralized, taking advantage of economies of scale. Some of their production sites have a capacity that is two to three times as large as the capacity in Dresden. Vandemoortele hoped to achieve its cost competitiveness in other ways. Having staked a claim in the European markets, Vandemoortele concentrated on its core business, i.e. the production on soy products, margarine and dough. The refinery firms it had acquired earlier on were sold. The company invested EUR 20 million in buildings and two completely new production plants with the most advanced technology in Europe, one of them in Dresden. Between 1993 and 1999 efficiency rose year by year.

The promising markets turned out to be highly volatile, however. In Dresden the Russian demand for margarine for instance fell from a peak of 70,000 tons in 1997 to 30,000 in 2006.

For the workforce, consisting of 140 employees in 1997, this meant radical reorganisation and regular waves of job losses. In view of technological change and fluctuations in demand, the company based its personnel policy on limited employment contracts as well as recruiting workers from temping agencies. Employees left when their contracts expired and they were no longer needed. Within the strategy of low cost mass production little attention was paid to the interests and attitudes of the workforce.

3   Foundations of involvement

In 1999 a consolidation period began. Technological efficiency gains were exhausted and subsequent investments were predominantly maintenance orientated. As demand and output fell, fixed production costs remained largely stable, thus leading to an increase in average costs. Management faced the challenge of raising efficiency by other means. In this phase the value of employees was discovered. The current plant manager of Vandemoortele Dresden, who took over then, found that downward pressure on wages and contingent work (limited contracts, temping, small-time contracts) should not be part of the company's cost minimization strategy and its reaction to sudden changes in demand.

3.1   Importance of job security

The new approach was partly owed to the specific demands of food production. Work in this industry requires a wide range of specific rules regarding cleanliness and hygiene and those rules can be taught and trained. However, it takes quite some time to internalize them so that e.g. washing or disinfecting hands, always wearing clean clothes and not sneezing into the machine becomes second nature, since any infection of the produce can mean the end of a company. Vandemoortele is very sensitive in terms of hygiene and invests heavily in information and in training to make sure that regulations are adhered to.

Employees on limited contracts have a relatively high turnover rate so that this investment does not always pay off. They may also feel under extra psychological pressure due to job insecurity distracting their attention from task requirements. When their time at Vandemoortele came to a close, employees tended to have high absence rates making life difficult for managers. When the job cuts in the wake of new technology had come to an end, management decided it was in Vandemoortele's best interest to offer its remaining 70 employees some job security through unlimited contracts gaining more stability in the workforce.

The other reasoning behind the shift to open-ended contracts was the plant manager's belief that only workers who feel safe and trust their management can be highly motivated. This is not a common view among managers in East Germany, an area with about 20% unemployment and plenty of highly qualified workers eager to find any kind of work. To a large extent employers are free to impose contracts with low pay, long hours and poor working conditions. Most of them take advantage of this situation by discouraging worker representation and avoiding co-determination.

Vandemoortele did not follow suit. The aim was not worker compliance. The Vandemoortele plant manager found that companies which cut wages tend to achieve cost reductions for a few years, but soon reach their limits and face an insecure and reluctant workforce. He believes that only satisfied and happy workers can be truly motivated and productive. The conflicts of interest between a profit maximizing employer and employees seeking rewarding employment are not brushed aside. Rather, it is emphasized that – in spite of those conflicts – there are large areas of common interest where both sides gain.

This requires a long-term employer-employee relationship through a high degree of job security and an integrated and consistent personnel policy with individual management instruments carefully tuned to work towards the same goal. What convinced the plant manager of the employee-centered approach were courses at business schools and management seminars whose message fitted well with his personal experience in the company. In his eyes, the greatest challenge is to gain and to maintain employee trust.

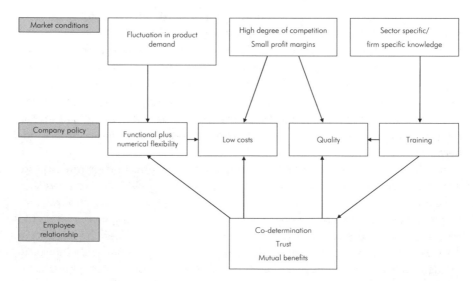

Figure 1. Company policy as a response to market conditions and the interests of employees

3.2 Trust through a works council

Economic theory gives some insight into the conditions under which employee involvement should come about (for a summary see Sadowski, Backes-Gellner & Frick, 1995). Normally, it would not be in the interest of employees to work towards more efficiency in the production process and to improve their firm-specific skills. Their own contribution might lead to a loss of working hours and a corresponding reduction in earnings or even dismissal, as can be demonstrated in a multitude of cases. On the other hand, efficiency and cost savings are paramount for the survival of the company and employees' own job security. Hence extra effort on the part of the workforce would pay off. To solve the dilemma, employees need to be able to influence management decisions to make sure that not just the employer gains with enhanced profits but that they, too, benefit from efficiency savings.

For that purpose, the institution of German-style works councils is invaluable. Elected by all employees for a period of four years to represent their interests in cooperation with management, councillors tend to have the trust of their colleagues. Works councils also inspire trust in the employer. Since many companies, especially in East Germany, have managed to prevent employees from setting up a works council (e.g. by intimidation and threat of plant closure) or to make it ineffective, the existence of a works council itself proves that employee concerns are taken seriously.

3.3 Decent pay and caring attitude

For German-style co-determination to develop its full potential, employees have to be convinced of the employer's good intentions and they need proof of it. Vandemoortele provided not only jobs with unlimited contracts; management also showed generosity in terms of pay. Faced by the option of leaving the German collective bargaining system, as many other companies in East Germany did, management continued to play by its rules keeping wages somewhat above the market rate. Accepting trade union influence, the second pillar of the German industrial relations system, is another trust-enhancing element in the worker-employer relationship.

The message that the company is honest and trustworthy becomes credible through consistency. Further policies signalling organisational support were introduced over the years. On top of decent wage rates employees can take advantage of a company pension scheme that is unique in East Germany. If employees invest a sum of up to one percent of their annual pay in their pension account, the company adds twice as much. Fees for training courses are paid for by the company if they are work related. Courses of no immediate benefit, such as language courses, get partly subsidized.

The caring attitude of management is also conveyed to newcomers as well as interest groups outside the company. Vandemoortele employs twice as many disabled workers as laid down by law, i.e. 10%. Whenever new employees are recruited from the job centre, the selection criteria are explicitly geared at disabilities that would not prevent the potential job holder from good performance. Disabled candidates, who often find themselves confronted with discrimination and rejection, are particularly grateful to have found a job and have proved to be more than up to their tasks. Their motivation and effort tend to be above that of the rest.

Emphasis on health and safety at Vandemoortele ensures that disabilities do not occur in the first place. Every day from autumn to spring employees are given an apple free of charge to remind them of the importance of vitamin C intake. They get a flu vaccination and a test for cancer of the bowels for free. Production workers have the technically most advanced ear plugs fitted to protect their hearing. Not only are employees invited to regular health information sessions with medical talks, but Vandemoortele also organizes an annual health and safety week with professional support and various events dedicated to certain risks such as smoking, unhealthy diet or stress.

3.4 Regular information

Economists that favour the German industrial system point out that employees who trust and feel attached to their company are more likely to make concessions when their employer faces a crisis. However, workers are also aware that managers may be opportunistic and could mislead them. Company bosses might talk up a crisis as a pretence to reduce labour costs and to boost their own profits. To prevent this, co-determination supplies the workforce with a stream of regular information.

The works council serves as the corner stone for an open culture at Vandemoortele. The plant manager invites the whole workforce to an afternoon information session once a week between shifts. This counts as work hours. He presents an overview of the contracts signed with customers to give an impression of the business climate. Other topics include efficiency problems and new developments. Also employees have the opportunity to make suggestions, ask questions and get a reliable answer.

Detailed information about the company situation and management policy, essential to build trust, is also crucial if workers are to work seriously toward cost reductions. Only when costs are known and employees are told exactly what they can do to influence them, are they able to contribute. During one of the weekly communication sessions the plant manager revealed the cost structure of Vandemoortele's products which so far had been treated as top secret in the company. In spite of the initial surprise at head office, this exception was tolerated.

Meetings between worker representatives and plant manager are held every month. Issues for the agenda come from both sides. As soon as managers are aware of an unresolved company problem from a management meeting, the issue is discussed with the works council, inviting suggestions and discussing alternative solutions. The goal is not to allow resentment or resistance to build up and to have concerns voiced as early as possible.

4 Policies of mutual benefit

The description of Vandemoortele's personnel strategy and its rationale so far has not answered the question where the efficiency savings that management has hoped for should come from. The generosity on the part of the company has ties attached. It is part of an exchange relationship with the workforce where both parties give and gain.

4.1 Numerical flexibility

Unlimited employment is what almost all employees want, but given the fluctuations in product demand at Vandemoortele, it poses a general problem. Since workers cannot easily be made redundant when orders run out, regular contracts may prove expensive unless adjustments are made through a flexible working time system. Vandemoortele offered unlimited employment contracts only to workers with good performance and combined those contracts with an

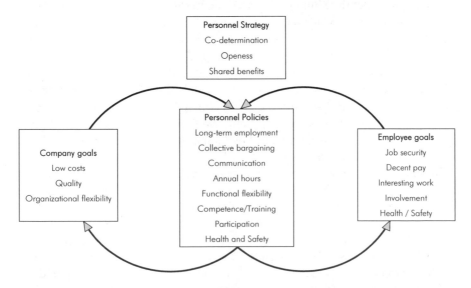

Figure 2. Integrated personnel policies reflecting employee and company goals

nual hours where employees work up to a maximum of 48 hours per week as and when necessary and have time off when output is low.

Employees gained a long-term perspective, a third of them working full-time and two thirds of them sharing the risk of falling product demand. For the majority of the workforce the company guarantees employment for only 80 percent of the regular number of annual hours product and provides the opportunity for employees to clock up more hours if product demand requires it. That way the risk of slack product demand is shared by employees and the company avoids paying overtime supplements.

4.2 Functional flexibility and training

Annual hours and a less than fully employed workforce have proved to be insufficient for keeping unit labour costs at Vandemoortele stable. The other method to respond to fluctuations in demand is functional flexibility. At Vandemoortele employees do not just replace absent colleagues in their department or fill gaps in insufficiently manned workplaces. With the approval and participation of the works council every employee is trained in two other tasks that differ significantly from their main occupation enabling them to step in when demand is unexpectedly high in another part of the company: Laboratory workers turn machine operators, machine operators are involved in computer work in the office or help out in the cold store, office workers are trained to stack pallets for instance. Employing seasonal workers becomes practically superfluous.

Training is expensive. But thanks to Vandemoortele's long-term commitment to the workforce this investment in a so-called "virtual internal labour market" is most likely to be paid back in terms of increased flexibility and efficiency. Just as importantly, the cross-over among office and production workers enhances the understanding of each others' task situation and the need for cooperation. It happens that employees call each other for help if necessary, without the supervisor having to put them into place. As a by-product, white and blue collar workers no longer sit apart during company parties. Communication among different groups of workers seems to have improved in various contexts. This is of further use to the company.

The benefit for the employees of the extra training lies partly in the "fun factor" of trying out something new and breaking the monotony of a regular job, which increases intrinsic motivation. In the long run, when workers might be looking for a different job this enhances their own value in the labour market. But they don't have to wait until then. Vandemoortele Dresden rewards the increased set of skills with bonus points. The more skills individual workers master, the more points they receive in terms of their value to the company and the safer they are should redundancies become unavoidable.

4.3   Virtual external labour market

To avoid dismissals, Vandemoortele set up another security device in accordance with the works council. It is called "virtual external labour market" and in some way functions like a temping agency. Workers whose labour is not required temporarily due to slack in demand are "loaned" to another company within a regional network of firms in the food industry. They remain employed at Vandemoortele but step in elsewhere when another firm is short of labour.

Firms in the food industry have similar hygienic requirements which take some time to learn. Correspondingly high training costs make temping by unskilled workers less suitable whereas employees commissioned by other food producers fit in without much introduction. In this way employees avoid redundancy and are subsequently able to return to their jobs. Employers save on the cost of emergency calls for extra labour or employee replacement costs if change in product demand proves only transient.

The introduction of the "external labour market" can serve as an example of how co-determination works at Vandemoortele. The idea of extending the internal labour market to outside firms in the food industry was mentioned to the works council as a possibility even before it had taken shape. It took two years to discuss it in this inner circle before it appeared workable and acceptable to employees. Only then was it introduced to the worker assembly.

The same process of systematically involving the works council is applied with other schemes including projects that are put forward and promoted by the employee side. At each step representatives have the opportunity give it a go or no-go. Ideas that survive this procedure are eventually wholeheartedly supported by the works council as well as the employees who can assume that their representatives would not agree to new policy measures that go against their interest.

4.4   Dismissal process

The most crucial and critical point of co-determination is its role in connection with dismissals which may still occur at Vandemoortele. When all flexibility enhancing mechanisms are exhausted and redundancies seem unavoidable in the eyes of management, this issue is put on the agenda of the subsequent works council meeting. The plant manager explains the situation, puts forward the alternative options considered and asks the works council members for their suggestions.

In the past, employee representatives have managed to come up with ideas management had not thought of, such as a flexible holiday scheme, which distributes the burden of insufficient work across the whole workforce. If the works

council cannot think of a way out of the problem, the next step is to confront
the employee assembly with the situation, again with the invitation to make
further suggestions. Solutions are still feasible. At one occasion some employees volunteered to work fewer hours or to take a few months' leave of absence,
thus preventing the looming redundancies.

Even if all attempts fail, the plant manager cannot be accused of ignoring alternative solutions to the problem. The rest of the procedure follows the labour
law and the candidates for dismissal are selected according to a list of criteria
previously agreed on in collaboration with the works council. The decision is
conveyed to the employees concerned by the plant manager in the presence of
a work council member. He still tries to be supportive offering his assistance in
finding a job elsewhere.

On the last occasion when three workers were dismissed, they quickly got
another job, two of them in one of the companies that form the network of the
"virtual external labour market". Again, the benefit of the safety net goes both
ways. The company saves some of the redundancy pay to which workers are
entitled according to their years of tenure by shortening the time of unemployment. On their part, employees can bridge their redundancy without loss of
income.

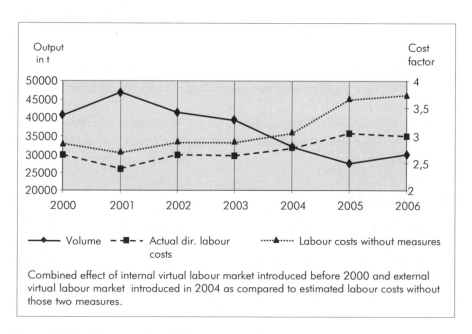

Combined effect of internal virtual labour market introduced before 2000 and external
virtual labour market introduced in 2004 as compared to estimated labour costs without
those two measures.

Figure 3. Development of unit labour costs in relation to output

5   Experiences with the management model

Each of the flexibility enhancing policies (4.1 to 4.3) helps Vandemoortele to reduce labour costs. The greatest proportion of savings is achieved through annual hours. The internal and the external virtual labour markets contribute further. Corresponding opportunity costs are shown in figure 3.

Savings are also derived from policies apparently geared at worker satisfaction, such as health and safety measures. Even in this case the gain for the company is considerable. EUR 5,000 to 7,000 spent on health and safety issues have led to a fall in absenteeism equivalent to a saving of EUR 60,000. Very rarely does such a small-scale investment in tangible assets yield a return of EUR 60,000 over a short time horizon. However, personnel-related savings are not even what contribute most to Vandemoortele's competitiveness since personnel represents only under 10% of overall costs in the industry. Raw materials, such as fat, energy and packaging have the much bigger weight of about 80% of costs.

5.1   Valuable suggestions

None of the cost factors are fixed. The amount spent on raw materials depends on how economically the production process is organized and how the workforce deals with those factors. The value of the Dresden plant chiefly lies in the trust and satisfaction of its employees and their commitment to care about, and contribute, to cost savings regarding the more important cost factor of raw materials, following the plant manager's motto: "If we pay properly for people's hands, we get their brains and minds free of charge."

At the beginning Vandemoortele triggered employees' ingenuity for cost reductions by financial incentives. The money became available by coincidence when administrative changes in the collective bargaining system led to a reduction in wage levels. Rather than lowering pay, as Vandemoortele would have been entitled, the sum of EUR 125 per month was labelled performance-related pay and could to be earned by employees contributing to cutting the waste of fat. It represents a major cost factor in margarine production and can be influenced by both production and office workers.

The effect was amazing. Over the years the waste of fat was reduced from 4% to 1%, which is the equivalent to nearly EUR 70,000. In 2005 employee suggestions produced cost savings of about half a million Euros, mainly through saving energy in the cold store. Head office was surprised. Not every suggestion is worth the cost incurred when turning it into practice. Well-meaning employees are often not aware of the technical implications of their ideas. Nevertheless management is careful to discuss every idea seriously and respect it as an expression of commitment that should not be discouraged by negative feedback.

5.2 Impact on competitiveness

Measurable financial returns on an impressive scale have helped overcome obstacles from Vandemoortele's head office. Investments in human resources are not normally very popular among managers who are trained to be engineers or experts of finance. While the purchase of new machines can be justified by subsequent cost savings, the rate of return from spending money on employees is difficult to predict and just as difficult to measure. Vandemoortele's executive did not always find open ears when arguing his position. It helped that the various management instruments partly financed themselves through the principle of give and take with employees and the amounts of money involved were not very large.

In the meantime there is little doubt that investment in long-term employee relationships and co-determination provide the best value for the company. Vandemoortele Dresden's achievements are displayed on the intranet to set an example for other production sites. The threat of plant closure and moving production to Poland or another Eastern European country where wages are much lower has vanished. The value of the Dresden employees with their high levels of commitment and felt responsibility for the competitiveness of the company is unique. Even though workers across the border are cheaper, an experiment with a joint venture in Poland showed that Vandemoortele would not be able to produce elsewhere at the same low level of overall costs.

The positive impact of worker involvement at Vandemoortele is no exception. Large-scale studies on the effects of co-determination demonstrate that the existence of a works council in large companies is associated with lower turnover rates, higher work productivity and higher wages than in equivalent work places without worker representation. Literature is ambiguous about the impact of works councils on competitiveness, however. Employee attitudes towards innovation do not seem to be affected by the institution as such, and in some studies the managers surveyed tend to perceive the influence of co-determination on profits as negative (Dilger, 2002).

5.3 Necessary and favourable conditions

The necessary conditions for employees to get involved with suggestions towards lowering costs is trust in management and the belief that company competitiveness is under threat. Workers in Dresden have little reason to be suspicious that the competition and potential crises evoked by management may not be real. Waves of past redundancies in their own company and current job losses at workplaces elsewhere remind them of the need for continuous adjustments.

The two main arguments used by economists against co-determination do not apply in their case: Entrepreneurs elsewhere may fear that the system gives employees so much power that they may claim an excessive share of company profits. The high unemployment rate in Saxony and Vandemoortele's international flexibility has kept the lid on employee demands. There is also no reason to believe that the system of co-determination may provide a protective shield over less productive workers, thus leading to adverse selection. Successive rounds of dismissals have left only the most competent and motivated workers behind.

Managers from other plants in Europe come to Dresden to see what measures could be adopted at their production sites. A similar policy elsewhere may not have the same impact, though. The employment situation in East Germany provides a backdrop that makes it difficult to transfer the system even to other Vandemoortele plants elsewhere in Europe. In other companies, depending on their history and the quality of the relationship between management and employees, trust may have to be built up over a long time. Financial investments in communication, training and motivation may not come as cheap as in Dresden. But as the Dresden example shows, getting employees involved, not through pressure or fear, but through satisfaction and information leads to outcomes many times over the input. To achieve this, managers are advised to adhere to certain rules.

6 Some dos and don'ts

Do	Don't
• set up policy principles supported by the workforce as well as management	• expect short-term employees to get involved at work
• adhere to mutually agreed policy guidelines • show respect for the work-related and personal qualities of your employees • listen actively • include employees and/or their representatives in problem solving early on	• forget that management measures need to provide benefits also for employees • underestimate the potential of employees • foster feelings of fear and insecurity • ignore the personal opinion of others • take unilateral decisions
• try to get feedback from employees	• go back on your word
• avoid preconceived notions and misunderstandings in communication	• change members of management frequently
• show that you care about the well-being of individuals • help employees to develop their personal potential	• accept that cost savings are limited • expect that management models can be fully translated to other companies
• point out career potential within the company	

7   Keeping momentum

As the cost structure becomes more favourable and more orders from customers are coming in, initiatives for cutting costs further are in danger of losing momentum. After so many efficiency drives the employees and managers involved at Vandemoortele may regard pursuing new ideas as troublesome and no longer very effective. Meanwhile the plant manager has run out of ideas for further improvements, but expects of continuous flow of suggestions for savings from enthusiastic employees. He regards it as most important that new ideas are not imposed from the top of the firm but that members of the workforce come up with suggestions. This way they would feel an even greater sense of ownership and responsibility. Especially if they see a benefit for themselves they might well be prepared to put in an extra effort.

To achieve that, everybody needs to be convinced that there is no limit to cost reduction, in the same way as human athletic achievements were raised over the years and have not come to a halt. The pressure is still on as competitors do not lack imagination and determination in cutting costs either. In future Vandemoortele will have to continue to identify areas of slack with potential to tighten efficiency. Currently there is no overseas competitor in the margarine market since cold storage would make long distance transports very expensive. However, overseas investors have already acquired refinery plants in Europe and they might take the next step of getting involved in margarine production.

So far there is no sign that even in the long run Vandemoortele Dresden with its participative approach to cost reduction would not be up to new competitors.

References

Dilger, A. (2002). Ökonomik betrieblicher Mitbestimmung – die wirtschaftlichen Folgen von Betriebsräten. München-Mehring.

Sadowski, D., Backes-Gellner, U., and B. Frick (1995). Works Councils: Barriers or Boosts for the Competitiveness of German Firms. British Journal of Industrial Relations, 3(3), 493-513.

Wenger, E. (1986). Freiwillig vereinbarte und erzwungene Organisationsregeln. Habil. TU München.

Website

http://www.Vandemoortele.com

Developing Business Excellence While Delivering Responsible Competitiveness

The case of Lloyds TSB

Nikos Avlonas and John Swannick

Abstract. There is a coherent business approach which brings together all facets of corporate responsibility – leadership, values, policy and processes, people, customers and society – to deliver improved performance. The EFQM Excellence Model helps us to:

- ensure we have a clear and constant purpose, it helps us to focus on the delivery of results.

- focus on customers and how we can create value by better meeting their needs.

- focus by systematically applying processes and fact-based assessments to manage our business and to make our strategic decisions.

- identify what we need to do to develop our people and maximise their potential.

- derive value from meeting our responsibilities to the communities we serve.

- achieve sustainable Excellence.

The EFQM CSR Framework, based on the EFQM Excellence model, is more suited to its purpose than other CSR specific frameworks as it more obviously:

- is business driven;
- aligns corporate responsibility with business strategy;
- aligns with balanced scorecard strategic and tactical priorities;
- delivers intrinsic internal and external benchmarking opportunities;
- facilitates stakeholder engagement at all levels of the organisation.
- links self-assessment, improvement activity and external reporting

The areas for improvement, identified in self-assessment against the Framework, are translated into prioritised objectives and key performance indicators developed to measure performance against these objectives. Working with colleagues across the business, bringing their particular knowledge and expertise to bear on the process, those objectives will inevitably reflect key business unit priorities.

The intention for Lloyds TSB is to deliver corporate responsibility performance that reflects the key strategic priorities of the business and aligns the organisation's corporate responsibility priorities with the business strategy to deliver value.

Key words: Excellence, Corporate Responsibility, Business Strategy, Performance, Value

1   A value based approach to corporate responsibility

Lloyds TSB is a major banking and insurance group, predominantly UK-based, but with operations in some 25 countries around the world. At the end of 2006, we were Europe's 13th largest bank by market capitalisation.

We have nearly 63,000 employees worldwide, serving a franchise comprising some 16 million personal and business customers. Our operation in the UK is probably the largest in terms of distribution reach, serving urban and rural communities through a network of over 2,000 retail outlets in addition to other mainstream channels such as Internet and telephone banking.

Since the merger between Lloyds Bank and TSB Group in 1996 we have more than doubled profits, built significant market shares in the provision of retail financial services, and our cross-selling ratio of products per customer is industry leading. In 2006, our post-tax return on average shareholders equity was 26.6%.

This has been accomplished against the background of a huge amount of change in the UK financial services industry. Competition is intensifying, and the UK financial services market is facing up to the impact of ever increasing regulation and price controls.

But managing a multi-billion pound operation comes from having total focus in what we do:

- strategies and governance that deliver sustainable business growth – profitable growth – for our shareholders;

- offering good products at the right price backed by a relentless pursuit of superior service and accessibility for customers;

- developing a committed and engaged workforce operating at recognised global high performance standards.

Against this backdrop, how exactly does corporate responsibility fit into our business strategy?

In our view, there are three approaches to corporate responsibility

- a way of doing business, ethically as a good corporate citizen. It's about a value system with an agenda being driven from the top and absorbed throughout the organisation...

- a disparate collection of policies and practices across different areas of business operation that have been brought together as part of an externally driven agenda to define a business' social responsibilities...

- conscious pursuit of a business strategy that recognises that the development of a brand and a reputation which reflects the expectations of all stakeholders will create real business value.

They are not mutually exclusive. They are three points on a continuum that take us from corporate philanthropy at one end of the spectrum to value-based corporations at the other, where external expectations demand a very hard focus on margin, productivity and investment performance.

That is the value-based approach to corporate responsibility: a business strategy that recognises that a brand and reputation, which reflect the expectations of all stakeholders, will create real business value. Corporate responsibility is no different from any other investment in the strategic assets and capabilities that drive business performance.

2   Integrating corporate responsibility in the business strategy

Our corporate vision is to make Lloyds TSB the best financial services company, first in the UK then across borders. Our CR strategy is to support our corporate vision by helping to build a great place for our people to work, a great place for our customers to do business, and generating great returns for our shareholders. In so doing, we believe we create value for all our stakeholders through:

- more effective risk management;

- enhanced brand perception, consideration and commitment;

- increased employee engagement;

- increased customer satisfaction;

- improved responsiveness to changes in patterns of customer behaviour;

- supporting development of new markets and innovation in existing markets;

- delivering competitive advantage through better corporate responsibility management.

There is a coherent business approach which brings together all aspects of managing stakeholder relationships and delivering value. We have been using the European Foundation for Quality Management's Excellence Model for some ten years. Its greatest value to us comes from the framework it provides:

- the model helps us to ensure we have a clear and constant purpose, it helps us to focus on the delivery of results;

- it helps us to focus on customers and how we can create value by better meeting their needs;

- it helps us to focus by systematically applying processes and fact-based assessments to manage our business and to make our strategic decisions;

- it also helps us to identify what we need to do to develop our people and maximise their potential;

- and it helps us to derive value from meeting our responsibilities to the communities we serve.

3   The EFQM Excellence Model

The EFQM Excellence Model is the most widely used organisational framework in Europe, being used by at least 30,000 organisations across more than 20 European countries. There are similar approaches in the United States and Japan. The EFQM Excellence Model is based on eight fundamental concepts of Excellence – a set of axioms that define excellence for European organisations. Corporate responsibility is one of these concepts: "Excellence is exceeding the minimum regulatory framework in which the organisation operates and to strive to understand and respond to the expectations of their stakeholders in society."

We know from the research amongst UK businesses conducted in 2005 by the University of Leicester for the EFQM and British Quality Foundation that companies which adopt and embrace the Excellence Model are more likely to create wealth and shareholder value than those that don't.

The research clearly demonstrates a direct relationship between the adoption of the Excellence Model and an improvement in overall business performance. The primary message is that the Excellence Model has a very important role to play in improving UK productivity and competitiveness but the opportunities are still not being exploited to the full. Key findings from the research include:

- when the principles of the EFQM Excellence Model are effectively adopted, performance improves in both the short and long term

- adopting the Excellence Model significantly enhances company value for all stakeholders.

- there is a strong and demonstrable link between effective deployment of the model and increased sales, business investment and shareholder returns.

- companies that adopt the Excellence Model successfully increase employment at a faster rate than comparison companies

- these significant financial benefits were seen over time indicating that excellence strategies have a lasting positive influence

4   The EFQM Framework for CSR

The EFQM Framework for CSR is an integrated approach that has the EFQM Excellence Model at its core. It focuses on stakeholder management and results, offering innovative tools for CSR assessment, evaluation, reporting and benchmarking.

The EFQM Framework for CSR is divided into the same nine criteria as the EFQM Excellence Model. The criteria are divided into *enablers* and *results*. The *enablers* – what an organisation does – cover leadership, people, strategy, partnerships and resources and processes. The *results* – what an organisation achieves – are separated into people, customer, society and business results.

The *enablers* are focused on stakeholder engagement and dialogue while the results are focused on organisational perceptions, CSR performance and stakeholder results. The criteria are sub-divided into areas of interest, topics, with guidance points on the issues covered under each topic.

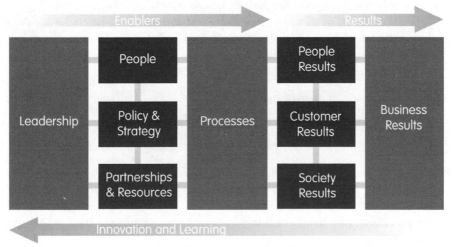

The EFQM Excellence Model is a registered trademark of EFQM

Figure 1. The EFQM framework

The EFQM Framework for CSR provides a complete CSR picture, while working within a framework that is about achieving organisational excellence. In essence, the EFQM Excellence Model is an organisational tool used to drive performance and continuous improvement, and the EFQM Framework for CSR signposts the key CSR fundamentals inherent in the tool.

The framework recognises that, although the outcomes of an organisation's social and environmental policies may belong, very properly, under society results, the successful implementation of those policies depends upon how well it performs in all of the criteria. It is affected by:

- the effectiveness of leadership at all levels of the organisation;

- alignment of the organisation's policy and strategy with its overall mission and vision;

- how partnerships and resources and processes are managed;

- the awareness and commitment of people, as well as the way they are managed.

Success can be quantified by measuring people, customer, society and key business results.

Together with the RADAR (Results, Approach, Deployment, Assessment & Review) scoring methodology, organisations are able to use the framework to assess themselves – to identify the strengths they should build on and the areas where they need to focus on improvement. Furthermore, the framework helps organisations to report performance by optimising the use of available information in a coherent approach which directly links inputs and outputs.

The identification of all the appropriate stakeholders and the understanding of their potential needs and expectations is a crucial starting point for organisations that want to be more socially responsible.

The EFQM Framework for CSR enables the organisation to:

- research who all the stakeholders are;

- understand what their expectations are;

- understand which measures are needed to meet these expectations.

It is a comprehensive, systematic and regular review by an organisation of its activities and results referenced. The self-assessment process allows the organisation to discern clearly its strengths and areas in which improvements can be made and culminates in planned improvement actions that are then monitored for progress.

The primary purpose of undertaking self-assessment is to better understand the status, the CSR maturity, of the organisation and to drive continuous improvement. It can be linked to other management processes within the organisation, primarily strategy development and business planning, particularly where the organisation uses a common approach to these processes.

The EFQM Framework for CSR is far more suited to its purpose than other emerging corporate responsibility specific frameworks as it more obviously:

- is business driven;
- aligns corporate responsibility with business strategy;
- complements balanced scorecard type approaches;
- delivers intrinsic internal and external benchmarking opportunities;
- facilitates stakeholder engagement at all levels of the organisation.
- links self-assessment, improvement activity and external reporting

The framework integrates CSR with stakeholder engagement in every activity and with many of the performance indicators of the organisation. It focuses not only on direct results, but also on the causes and how to get there. And, since it is a management framework, not a standard, organisations can easily integrate existing standards (e.g. ISO 9000 and ISO 14000) into the framework.

Lloyds TSB has been integrally involved in development of the EFQM Framework for CSR. It was represented on the working group which devised it and was the first organisation to test it through high-level self-assessment, in 2003.

There were a number of drivers behind Lloyds TSB's involvement.

1. The value-based approach which it takes to corporate responsibility dictates that the company's corporate responsibility strategy should be aligned with the strategic focus of business. That means that the corporate responsibility management model had to fit with the primary means of driving the company's strategic and tactical priorities – the Balanced Scorecard. The EFQM Excellence Model and the EFQM Framework for CSR are ideally suited as the model is, in itself, a balanced scorecard and there are clear synergies in the stakeholder focus of both approaches.

2. Lloyds TSB's corporate responsibility steering group of senior executives clearly wanted to develop a corporate responsibility management system that could be integrated throughout business and owned by individual business units rather than the central Corporate Responsibility team. Firstly, this reflected the complexion of the steering group which, although including heads of relevant functional disciplines such as Human Resources, Risk Management and Investor Relations, is fundamentally led by business unit leaders. Secondly, it ensured that responsibility is devolved throughout the business to key line management. Widespread familiarity with the EFQM Excellence Model across the organisation, its fit with the Balanced Scorecard and the essential business nature of the Framework, facilitated this objective.

3. The company had ground-breaking and award-winning programmes in corporate responsibility areas such as training and people development, equality and diversity, work-life balance and community investment. But it recognised that this was not enough and had already identified the need for a systemic approach which meant both developing programmes in areas where it was not as strong and creating a commitment to continuous improvement where it was. This involved identifying and incorporating a range of corporate responsibility Key Performance Indicators (KPIs) across the business building on existing Balanced Scorecard objectives within individual business units. Working with individual business units to identify and implement improvement activity against agreed KPIs is inherent in the broad-based self-assessment and improvement focus of the EFQM approach.

5   Implementing the EFQM approach

In 2004, the group's corporate responsibility team undertook a full-company self-assessment against the framework. In 2005, a number of representatives from key business units contributing to the group's corporate responsibility profile participated in a more comprehensive self-assessment. We identified areas for improvement which have been built into the balanced scorecard priorities of the corporate responsibility team. They included:

- Undertaking a self-assessment across the business against the EFQM Framework for CSR.

- Use existing data collection processes to inform the self-assessment

- Use existing data collection processes to inform the self-assessment and relate to external reporting

- Analyse performance and perception of performance against the framework and identify strengths and key areas for improvement.

- Identify improvement priorities and improvement activity that aligns with Balanced Scorecard objectives for each business unit.

- Set Key Performance Indicators and targets based on these priorities aligned with specific target measures under the Balanced Scorecard of individual business units.

- Review progress with business unit on an ongoing basis and globally with the Corporate Responsibility Steering Group.

- Share results and progress with relevant networks of employees throughout the business, to both highlight achievements and gain buy-in to supporting improvement activity in individual business units.

- Using the EFQM Excellence Model, facilitate effective benchmarking of performance with other organisations across industries and sectors.

One of those priorities was to formalise a network of senior managers across the business who report into members of the group's Corporate Responsibility Steering Group and could assume responsibility for local implementation initiatives. Around 40 individuals were identified and in March 2006, based on 2005 performance, 28 of this 'enablers' network' undertook the most in-depth self-assessment yet against the EFQM Framework for CSR, validated by CSE Associates, EFQM licensed consultants.

One of the outputs of the self-assessment was Lloyds TSB's 2005 corporate responsibility report. Another was areas for improvement, identified in the self-assessment, to be translated into prioritised objectives and the development of KPIs to measure performance against these objectives. Working with colleagues across the business, bringing their particular knowledge and expertise to bear on the process, those objectives inevitably and desirably reflected key business unit priorities: That Lloyds TSB deliver corporate responsibility performance which reflects the key strategic priorities of the business and aligns the organisation's corporate responsibility priorities with the business strategy and priorities of individual business units.

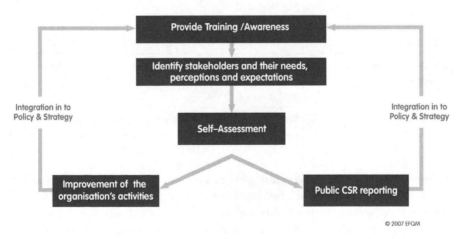

Figure 2. EFQM implementation framework

From the 2006 self-assessment a whole range of Areas for Improvement were identified – 12 key areas in total and a number of dovetailing priorities under each area. These are shown in the table below.

Table 1. Areas for improvement

Areas	Objectives
Targeted internal communications programme	Develop CR content in all internal communications channels and establish business unit champions amongst CR steering Group and Enablers' network.
Ensure managers understand how CR fits with business as usual	Build the business case for corporate responsibility with specific case study evidence to demonstrate application across the business.
Promote employee CR proposition	Shift internal perceptions from basic CR awareness and understanding, through commitment and engagement. to build employee advocacy.
Develop CR management system	Use enablers' self-assessment and areas for improvement to develop agreed balanced scorecard objectives and resultant Key Performance Indicators.
Local stakeholder engagement	Develop best practice resources to support local activity and leverage existing commitments.
Build our financial inclusion programme	Support research to increase sustainability of community finance schemes and enhance commercial attractiveness of sector.
Review CR contribution to business tender process	Work with Corporate Relationship Managers to develop CR contribution to business tenders and pitches.
Enhance CR aspects of procurement process	Work with Group Procurement to implement ethical purchasing policy and review contribution to environmental performance.
Develop Climate Change strategy	Review carbon management programme, environmental performance indicators and develop targets.

In early 2007, the CR team undertook a series of review meetings with enablers to review progress against the identified areas for improvement. Progress against the objectives is detailed in the relevant sections of this report. From this review, and the self-assessment incorporating review evidence undertaken in March 2007, we have now developed a coherent set of strategic focuses to frame our primary objectives and actions going forward. These are:

- CR management development;
- better communication;
- focused key stakeholder engagement;
- confronting climate change;

- increasing financial inclusion;
- supporting brand positioning.

6   Results

Already we are seeing significant results from this process in our key focus areas:

6.1   Communication

Fundamental to our communications strategy is the belief in a corporate responsibility business case premised on the impact of our CR reputation on employee engagement. That is, not just in terms of employees' perception of our social, environmental and ethical performance but, equally, in a greater understanding of how that responsibility is a feature of all our business operations. This employee 'CR proposition' recognises that effective communication of the link between business strategy and CR priorities will increase employees' awareness and understanding and ultimately raise levels of engagement, commitment and advocacy of the organisation as both an employer and provider of financial services.

In September 2006, as part of our communication segmented by stakeholder audience approach, we published an employee-focused CR report for the first time. *Workout* reflected the key CR issues our employees told us they thought important in a series of focus groups in 2005 – responsible lending, people development, local community engagement and the environment – in a lively and engaging format. It was published as a supplement to our employee magazine, UpFront and circulated to all employees.

Upfront magazine itself is published monthly and contains a range of features and news stories on key CR events and issues. It builds on a daily intranet news service, UpFront News, which featured over 250 CR related news stories in 2006. These 'bulletin' news stories are supplemented by extensive CR information, regularly updated, on the group's corporate responsibility intranet site which is also linked to CR information on other business units' intranet sites.

Our customer CR leaflet, 'honest, trustworthy.....who cares?', containing case studies of our commitment to various stakeholder groups, was available from branches throughout 2006 and by early 2007, nearly 200,000 had been distributed.

6.2   Stakeholder engagement

Our interaction with communities through local opinion formers, community organisations, local authorities, as well as major local employers and the wider business community, is a critical platform for developing our brand and reputation with key stakeholder groups.

An estimated 20,000 Lloyds TSB employees are involved with these local stakeholder organisations in some form. For example, we employ around 1,500 school governors and hundreds of local councillors and magistrates. Much is represented by personal volunteer activity but there is also significant interaction on behalf of the company or in time supported by the company.

Some of the relationships are based on operational issues – maintaining our 'license to operate' as a local business. Others reflect local business development priorities – the development of business introducer networks or building profile in critical local markets, for example.

Supporting local stakeholder engagement was a key CR objective for 2006. Over the year we have undertaken both qualitative and quantitative research amongst local branch directors, senior business managers and Corporate Bank relationship directors. This has allowed us to develop a simple diagnostic tool for local managers to identify their own priorities, and a database of case studies illustrating the wealth of business best practice across the group.

We have also supported personal development activity in this area. The leadership and management curriculum of the University for Lloyds TSB includes a range of courses which can include short-term 'secondments' or interim management 'consultancy' with external organisations. The approach is designed to both test individuals' skills and competencies in a different environment and provide performance development in key stakeholder engagement approaches including networking and influencing skills. In 2006, such courses were part of the support to those people in the organisation moving from managing 'self' to managing others and managing managers.

6.3   Climate change

The UK Government has stated its belief that climate change is the greatest long-term challenge facing the world today. Measures to tackle climate change will have potential implications for regulation, taxation and public policy and will carry both risks and opportunities for companies and the public.

In respect of our own direct environmental impacts, our immediate priority is to reduce our carbon emissions. We have introduced a five-year carbon management programme, which, through a series of energy saving projects and other initiatives, will reduce our carbon footprint. We have a target to reduce property-related emissions and identified other opportunities in relation to waste reduction and business travel.

While our direct carbon intensity is relatively low compared to other industry sectors, we still need to fully understand the potential financial impact of climate change on others that we may lend to or invest in, so that we can manage the risks and identify business opportunities. We established a group-wide Climate Forum, led by the deputy group chief executive, to develop a holistic approach to managing climate-related risks and opportunities.

Using 2002 as the baseline, we have set a target to reduce our CO_2 emissions by 30% by 2012. Having set this reduction target, we will offset those emissions we cannot reduce, commencing in 2007. This will make our operations carbon neutral.

6.4 Financial inclusion

Community finance initiatives offer a range of loans covering diverse requirements from debt refinancing, to home improvements and business start-ups. We have supported a number of the early pilots with staff secondments and funding, using our expertise to develop appropriate processes. Lloyds TSB has also been involved in a wide range of projects on both a commercial and semi-commercial basis, providing capital for loan funds which are on-loaned to business start-ups, micro-business and social enterprises.

With our involvement in Change London, the Local Investment Fund, Bridges Community Ventures Fund, South Coast Money Line and Hampshire Community Banking Partnership, Lincolnshire Loan Fund, One London Limited, Wessex Development Fund, Prime, South West Investment Group, and Arrow Fund, around GBP 10 million was committed to the sector in 2006. This is in addition to our normal commercial lending direct to small businesses in the most deprived areas.

South Coast Money Line (SCML) is a community development finance institution, providing a mix of unsecured personal and micro-enterprise loans, and home improvement loans which are secured. This year, SCML launched a financial capability initiative called 'Smart Money' to provide money and budgeting skills. SCML also provided a lead role in the development of a Community Banking Partnership for South Hampshire, in partnership with Portsmouth Housing Association and Lloyds TSB who are funding a project manager.

The SCML model of working in partnership to deliver a comprehensive financial inclusion project is also helping them become financially sustainable. Since commencing trading in May 2000, SCML has lent customers loans to the value of GBP 2 million. For the financial year ending March 2007, SCML will generate sufficient income from interest income and other contractual relations to cover up to 70% of its operating costs. These contracts are with housing associations, local authorities and Government. SCML now operates, either by directly delivering services or in partnership with sub-contractual arrangements, in Hampshire, Devon and Sussex. To improve their sustainability still further SCML is working with the original funder Lloyds TSB and Community Finance Solutions from the University of Salford.

In 2006 we set up a Financial Inclusion Fund to finance research and development activities in promoting the long-term sustainability of community finance and enhance the commercial attractiveness of lending to the sector.

6.5 Brand positioning

By the end of 2006, the group's refreshing of its brand positioning saw the development of our 'For the journey.....' concept. This underpins the long-standing commitment in our Group Code of Business Conduct (see www.lloydstsb.com/corporate_responsibility) to maintaining long-term relations with our customers and the premise that honesty and integrity in our dealings with customers are prerequisites for a sustained and successful relationship. This, and Lloyds TSB's sponsorship of the 2012 London Olympic and Paralympic Games, with its legacy issues around economic regeneration, skills development social inclusion, community investment and youth, offers a tremendous platform for increasing the contribution of corporate responsibility to Lloyds TSB's brand identity.

References

European Foundation for Quality Management (2003) "EFQM Excellence Model", available at www.efqm.org

European Foundation for Quality Management (2004). "The EFQM Framework for CSR", available at www.efqm.org

Centre of Quality Excellence, University of Leicester (2005). © EFQM and BQF, "Organisational excellence strategies & improved financial performance" available at www.quality-foundation.org.uk

R S Kaplan and D P Norton "The Balanced Scorecard: Measures that drive performance", Harvard Business Review, January-February 1992, 71-79

Kaplan and Norton, "The Balanced Scorecard: translating strategy into action, Boston: HBS Press, 1996

Lloyds TSB (2007). „Corporate Responsibility Report 2006", available at www.lloydstsb.com/about_ltsb.asp

Lloyds TSB (2004). "Group code of business conduct", available at www.lloydstsb.com/about_ltsb.asp

Trying to Understand Management Models

An explorative inquiry into the nature and functionality of management models

Jan Jonker, Michel van Pijkeren, and Jacob Eskildsen

Abstract. In the previous chapters a number of management models have been presented. What ties them together is the fact that companies have created them in order to address present and future organisational challenges. We have chosen to show them as they are, with as much as possible respect to differences in cultural, contextual and linguistic backgrounds. Now that this volume comes to a close, this final chapter will be used to shed some light on the nature of the models presented previously. We therefore set out to explore their character and functionality, thus enabling to identify what these models have in common but also how they can be distinguished from each other. Our aim of this exploration is to grasp the more fundamental, conceptual and theoretical aspects of management models. This exploration is guided by a number of questions. How can management models be classified and categorised? What principles are underpinning? What role do these models play in organisations and what are different functions they might have? All these questions drill down to: "which theoretical perspectives can be distilled when analysing the models presented in this volume?" For sure we will not be able to elaborate all these questions in detail although we do hope that the results will establish the foundations for further investigation – be it more theoretical or more practical.

Key words: organising, interactionism, complexity

1 Introduction: Past, present and future of organisations

The management models presented in this volume cover a wide range of issues and aspects within the sphere of organisations. They aim to support organisations in coping with the needs and expectations of stakeholders in their double-context: business and society. The contemporary business enterprise is not only involved in the business context but is by its sheer size, resources and power involved in societal developments that didn't seem to be the business of business before. But without even soliciting this role, organisations have become dominant actors within society. Their impacts are reaching far beyond the economic spheres of life. As such they arouse admiration and hope for a better future, but also feelings of resentment, distrust and blame for diverse problems, such as climate change, social inequality, use of scarce resources, copyrighting natural DNA for commercial purposes and long-term pollution. Given the current prominence of business organisations, a growing array of enquiries on how they should function – heard louder then ever before – becomes apparent. In coping with these, often conflicting, demands organisations are pressured to construct innovative organisational concepts and management practices taking these demands into account in a balanced way. On the one hand the context in which organisations operate has moved from mono-dimensional to multi-dimensional. On the other hand the processes within and across the boundaries of the organisation have become increasingly complex and variable. When taken together management has the task to cope with a growing complexity in a flexible and transparent manner. One of the ways organisations deal with this challenge is to construct management models. As such they are frames of choice showing what is being taken into account and what not. They are tools guiding actions. A closer look demonstrates that management models are omnipresent within organisations and in discussions concerning the future direction of organisations. In some way they seem to support the process of managing complexities, of learning and providing a sense of direction. Despite their presence, however, little is known about what these models actually are, how they can be described and what their role is within organisations. We therefore think it is relevant to present an academic elaboration on the nature and functionality of management models. We will then use this clarification to review the 12 models presented previously. We'll continue to outline some trends and developments that present organisational challenges for the future. We will close by pointing out some further developments be it within organisations and or academic research.

2   Organising and value creation

Business organisations are deliberate social constructions aiming to create value for their stakeholders. If they don't create value, they soon cease to exist. Value creation encompasses organising the transformation of e.g. human and natural capitals into values. In the transformation process a blend of capitals are transformed into outputs that are valued higher than the separate values invested. In the actual process of transformation collaboration, structure and relations are central elements. Organisations can thus be seen as deliberate constructions based on social relations leading to the organisation of this transformation process. Organisations do so by establishing, maintaining and facilitating relatively stable relations among actors. Within these relations, actors collaborate based on complementary competences and a sense of common interest. Thus organising can be considered to structure collaboration in order to transform inputs into outputs. These relations are build around the focal point of value creation; the purpose of organising.

We will focus on the process of organising here instead of the 'construct' organisation. We do so because the organisation is predominantly associated with rather static attributes such as buildings, technology, products and structures. We believe the phenomenon organising has other fundamental characteristics that seem to be more relevant in contextualising and explaining management models. Organising draws attention to the dynamic aspects of interaction, sense making, building relations and transforming. Currently, organising takes place in an increasingly dynamic environment requiring organisations to become almost real change agents. In order to adapt and change, organisations need to focus more on these dynamic and often unpredictable, social aspects. Precisely these aspects will be elaborated in further sections. We believe that the nature and functionality of management models are best explained if they are considered to be part of the organising process.

3   Modelling organising

When organising is considered to enable value creation through structured and focused collaboration, how can we explore this phenomenon? Organising is one of the inherent qualities of mankind that distinguishes its kind from (other) 'animals'. By reflecting on this organisational quality certain characteristics – or elements – appear. In the following we will outline four of these characteristics of organising. These provide the building blocks of a generic model[1] that further down will be used to reflect in a more systematic manner on the nature and functionality of management models that are presented in this volume.

3.1   Acting

Organising is action oriented. People organise themselves through a continuous stream of acts of themselves, or others, to get things done. When people organise they inherently act towards a desired future, a goal. They set things, themselves and other people in motion in order to transform inputs into out-

---

[1] There are of course many other generic management models. Just to name a few: the 7S's models, or Porters Value Chain or the EFQM Model. All these models provide a vision towards one or more aspects of what is called organising. The model closest to what we present here is the so-called PDCA Cycles. PDCA stand for Plan Do Check Act a can be characterised as a circular approach to individual and collective action. This cycle can be found in the literature regarding quality management.

puts. By acting, people take hold of their own environment, using available resources and competencies, creating what is of value to them. Through their acts
they establish (some) control over their situation. What first and foremost happens when organising takes place is that the individual actions of people are
connected and coordinated into collective action. That is where the 'power' of
organising is emerging since collectivism implies complementarity in acting towards a goal that is perceived as being common.

3.2   Envisioning

Acting, which is fundamental to organising, is furthermore focussed. In organising actions are undertaken deliberately towards a shared – although abstract –
goal. Envisioning a goal helps to focus the actions of people who are involved
in what needs to be organised and how it could be achieved. This goal may be
explicit or rather implicit. Still it serves to create a sense of direction, belonging
and purpose. The goal of organising is defined within a certain context. Organising takes place in, and is to some degree dependent, on the interaction with
other actors and groups. Organising is not a goal in itself. It lies in contributing
to something or someone outside the organisation itself. The case of the Triodos bank for example shows an organisation that envisions making sustainable
enterprises possible by offering financial solutions.

3.3   Reflecting

The process of organising takes place within a certain context. Those involved
in the actions towards certain goals operate within boundaries. The context or
environment nevertheless, interacts with, and affects the organisation across

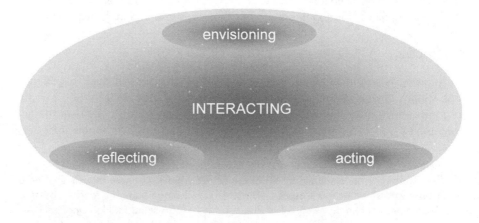

Figure 1. A model of organising

these boundaries. The goals and actions need to fit the context and needs and expectations of the actors in that context. Assuring this fit means that organising involves reflecting on the way goals and actions fit in the context. Reflecting has both an internal and an external orientation; internal reflection focuses on the control if envisioned goals are achieved, external reflection focuses on the fit with contextual developments and expectations.

3.4 Interacting

The final aspect of organising encompasses structuring and ordering the three aspects introduced above. Structuring the processes of envisioning, acting and reflecting is based on interacting. Interacting is fundamentally grounded in communication. Interacting is crucial to organising and serves to:

- Connect people to one another and share ideas. As such interaction – based on communication – is a prerequisite for collective action. If people are not connected to one another given the goal at hand, actions go in diverse directions. It is exactly the combined effort of actions that enable the realisation of goals.

- Construct a shared cognitive map. The cognitive map of an organisation is the informal frame of reference stating what is appropriate and what is not. In the language people use it becomes clear how reality is perceived. This leads to a particular way in which an organisation conceives of external and internal issues and utilises strategies to cope with these issues. As such it institutionalises a way of decision making, which is to perceive phenomena and respond to these in an informed manner. How to perceive them and subsequently what this implies is framed in a language that is consistent with the cognitive map of an organisation.

- Set the boundaries of organising. By envisioning it is defined what is within the organisation and what is not, simply because language addresses certain issues, and others not.

Interacting is thus the structuring constituent that aligns organisational processes into a sensibly stable configuration of collective action. It is so to speak the 'oil' that makes the processes of envisioning, acting and reflecting come together and flow. This view on organising is represented in the model shown in the figure above[2].

---

[2] We have deliberately omitted to draw lines and arrows between the various elements or characteristics. It goes without saying that the elements are firmly intertwined and that in our view interaction is the key-element that binds the other three. But to say that one them has a more dominant role would lead to a picture with suggestions of relations that are not defendable.

3.5   Integrating through interacting

Organising can be seen as connecting and aligning the organisational processes of envisioning a certain goal, acting to work towards this goal and reflecting if acting results in the envisioned goal. These processes are connected through continuous interaction. This incessant stream of interaction gradually forms an established pattern. This pattern becomes apparent in for example strategy statements, organisational systems and processes for production, quality requirements and settings for e.g. logistics, technology or human resources. Through all these interactions people increasingly give meaning to these aspects of organising. People interact through the use of different media and the linguistic repertoire that is available. The linguistic repertoire consists of the different ways language is used in organising. It can be outlined as follows:

- verbal accounts consist of conversations between members and stories being told. In these conversations and stories people for example express ideas, make decisions and give orders. By using verbal language people directly connect to one another and set things in motion.

- non-verbal accounts are the non-spoken acts through which people express themselves. Non-verbal communication determines to a large extend how the content is transferred.

- textual accounts are the written documents flowing through an organisation. These can have the functionality of transferring and confirming ideas.

- visual accounts are pictorial representations of artefacts or ideas. Visual accounts can be both realistic as well as abstract. Visuals have the quality to simplify real world phenomena and make it easy to understand and communicate these.

So far we have tried to show in the above that organising takes place because of value creation. Value creation takes place in transformation processes. Organisations can be seen as deliberate constructions based on social relations leading to the organisation of this transformation process. Organising necessitates people to interact in order to establish dedicated and suitable patterns of envisioning, acting and reflecting. Patterns that 'fit' the goal of the organisation and are aligned with the needs and expectations of internal and external stakeholders. In order to create these patterns constantly choices have to be made. The configuration of these choices leads to a business or organisational strategy[3].

---

[3]   We assume here that the fulcrum of organising is making choices in the light of available resources (the capitals) based by definition on a subjective interpretation of the impact of intentional actions in a dynamic context. Where there are choices, always more can be made given the resources etc.. The choice of choices is generally

In order to make the proper choices people within organisations use different modes of a linguistic repertoire when interacting with each other. This interaction is based upon – but can also lead to – a dedicated management model. One that makes sense for the people involved when it comes to making choices regarding actions. The model in Figure 1 will be used to explore the functionalities of management models. The next section will elaborate this.

4 Models and organising

Management models can be characterized as simplified representations or 'images' of a dynamic organisational reality in which a multitude of choices are present. The word 'management' however, is a bit confusing here, because, while these models aim to provide guiding principles for action in a generic manner, they often do not provide 'instructions for use'. Taking a closer look they aim to visualise and describe an interpretation of an infinite complex and 'fuzzy' phenomenon – since that is the reality of organising. But by constructing models actors are enabled to create common understanding of this 'to be organised' phenomenon through collective processes of sense making. The result of this often iterative and collaborative process is a 'picture' naming and framing those elements that seem to be of importance to the (organisational) actors involved. The process of creating a management model is therefore in all probability more important then the actual result. While the result is a picture or diagram almost always illustrated with words and the relations between them, it is in this process that the people involved have to give meaning to different – often qualitative and broadly typified – complex mental (and) (or) actionable constructs. Drilled down to its bare essence the 'product' of this process is a contextual interpretation of what matters, here and now. What matters differs for every organisation and changes over time. Their life cycle depends on the ability to adapt to the variability of the context in which the organisation operates.

Management models are viewed here as a means to interact, as part of the linguistic repertoire managers and other people inside and outside the organisation can use. Typically they consist of a picture combining textual and visual elements. This picture then represents the way matters at hand are perceived and interpreted. It enables a 'structured' form of interaction facilitating in turn the understanding of relevant issues among people. They also help to translate issues for different stakeholders. To further explore the different functionalities of management models we will use the model presented earlier. We will try to

---

called 'equifinality'. Strategies emerge out of actions but at the same time people can make fundamental choices beforehand leading to a restraint set of choices, which in hindsight can be labelled as a strategy. Management models can be seen as 'menus of choices' without specification of the precise actions to be taken.

show how models facilitate the interaction among people connecting the processes of envisioning, acting and reflecting:

1. A management model can be used to translate a vision internally. This helps to guide actions on the ground. It also facilitates the translation of the vision externally in order to communicate a desired image among stakeholders;

2. A model can be used to create an understanding of how to structure collective acting. It does so by arranging complex issues and developments in a visual representation of specific elements and their relations. The model is then used to reduce complexity and enables informed decision-making;

3. Finally a model can be used to monitor if envisioned goals are being achieved and if these still match the needs and expectations of stakeholders given a particular context.

What we conclude from the sections above is that organising aims to create value for the stakeholders involved by transforming capitals. Organising this process involves envisioning a goal, acting toward this goal and reflecting on the way acting actually leads to realising this envisioned goal. All this involves relentless choice making. Through their interactions people gradually connect these fundamental elements of organising. In our opinion organising takes place in the process of organising. Management models are part of this complex interaction between people. They have the function of [1] translating the vision, [2] help to create an understanding of how to act and [3] monitoring if the goals are being achieved. Baring this concise taxonomy of functionalities in mind, the models in the book will be reviewed below.

5   Management models in practice

In this section we will briefly review the presented management models in order to elaborate on their functionalities. For every model we will describe what the model entails and what according to our interpretation its function and role is in the organisation. The taxonomy is used to elaborate on the various functionalities.

5.1 Cilag AG

At Cilag qualitative and quantitative models are created and currently in use. As is shown the qualitative models set a vision and normative reference for all employees. The corporate credo and the standards of leadership clearly state what the organisation stands for and what is expected of its employees. These models aim to translate the vision of Johnson and Johnson in its subsidiaries. The quantified models presented have a complementary, yet different functionality; they aim to assist managers in taking informed and founded decisions. The models do not envision some desired future state, but seek to mimic real life. This is done by framing key elements in the organisation and relating these elements through mathematic formulas into causal loops. The models create a decision environment for manager where they can test 'what if' propositions and simulate the outcomes. The models thus seek to support the decision making processes control operations.

5.2 Henkel

The model deployed by Henkel structures its initiatives in the area of corporate social responsibility. The model aims to involve employees and pensioners into social projects. As such Henkel establishes broader and richer relations with the communities in which they operate. The models determine the lines of authority for the initiative and structure their focus areas. The models do not aim to indicate causal relationships between elements but attempt to give a clear overview of organisational structure and focus areas. Along with the visualised values and principles the models constitute a frame of reference for those involved with Henkel. The models serve to illustrate internally and externally what activities are undertaking and how these are embedded within the organisation. The model visualises how the values are put into practice. As such the models aim to translate a vision of how to operate.

5.3 Danske Bank

The Danske Bank uses a quantitative model elaborating the relations within its value chain. The model underscores the business case for sound human resource management. It specifies and quantifies the relations between employee motivation and customer loyalty and financial results. As such it supports managers in making informed decisions on human resource policies. The model reduces the noise and complexity of the relation between intangible assets and the financial bottom line into quantified, easy to grasp measures. It serves to monitor the tangible outcomes of activities in the field of human resource management and gives managers handles to initiate the proper activities.

5.4 AgroFair

The AgroFair differs from the other cases because it is based on a unique model of ownership and vertical integration. The model represents how ownership and vertical integration are structured within the organisation. In order to cope with the developments of (1) growing consumer concern about social and environmental issues and (2) increasing economies of scale AgroFair initiated a revolutionary ownership model. The model arranges co-ownership of producers which are in the conventional supply chain marginalised by the sheer market power of the main food traders and wholesalers. The model presents a framework which shows internally and externally how the organisation is structured. As such the model can be classified as a translation of the AgroFairs' vision. Internally it supports the communication about the roles and responsibilities in the organisation. Externally the model shows how the distinctive organisational vision is structured.

5.5   Gaz du France

Since Gax du France was confronted with the opening up of the energy markets of France and Europe in general it initiated a global change of its management model in order to cope with the demands of a multinational corporation. The newly introduced model seeks to support the establishment of responsible management practices throughout the corporation. These practices need to be responsive and aligned to the local circumstances and cultural factors. In order to realize this the management model ProMaP is implemented. This model seeks to support local managers to implement innovative and responsible management practices by establishing a reference framework of group wide best-practices. It furthermore measures improvements and benchmark these throughout the group. The model is typically seeks to create and increase an understanding of best practices and to monitor if the actual practices achieve the desired results.

5.6   ABN AMRO Real Bank

The model deployed by the ABN AMRO Real Bank was created in order to make sense of contextual factors: the societal conditions in Brazil and the corporate values that were formulated and implemented. The model translates the broad vision of "becoming a sounder bank for a sounder society" into clearly demarcated areas. The model which only broadly outlines the vision is very much the beginning of a host of initiatives. It supports the organisation to create an awareness of sustainability issues and gives guidance on 'what to organise'. On the other hand the model stays silent on 'how to organise' or how to monitor these initiatives. In the development of the model, however, performance indicators have been formulated. But how these indicators influence decision making processes is not determined by the model at hand.

5.7   Post Danmark

Post Denmark underwent fundamental change in the last decade in order to develop from a governmental agency to a commercial viable company. In order to structure this process and develop a completely new management approach several models have been constructed and used. The TIQ model (total involved in quality) and the strategy map serve to translate the vision for the future into concrete activities. They show which basic elements are needed and how concrete activities are derived from these building blocks. The organisation furthermore uses the EFQM model to reflect on its operations from a holistic perspective. The EFQM model is used to self-assess the status of development of organisational aspects. In concordance with the EFQM model the key processes within the organisation are mapped in order to enhance the understanding of manager how to steer and control process quality. The results from these processes are furthermore monitored using an established model of customer satisfaction. In short the models in use by Post Danmark together embody all the functionalities proposed in our taxonomy.

5.8   Water Corporation Western Australia

Right from its conception the Water Corporation of Western Australia headed the fundamental challenge of a declining water supply. In order to address this challenge and to organise a sustainable solution, the organisation introduced a management model comprising of 18 business principles. Half of principles are focusing on processes and the other half on outcomes. This model is used to implement the sustainability strategy throughout the company. The model supports employees in making decision by framing how to act and which overriding goals need to be achieved. The model seeks to translate a broad vision, on the way a diverse set of capitals (human, financial, manufactured and natural) is transformed to create value, internally and externally. As such the model forms a frame of reference that steers and guides organisational behaviour.

5.9   Triodos Bank

The model applied by the Triodos Bank outlines a vision of what the organisation stands for and how it seeks to contribute to its wider context. It describes the different levels of organising and the roles that are distinguished in order to achieve the vision. It is predominantly a model that fuels the dialogue about the way members play their part in the organisation. It clarifies the expectations of management towards its employees by sketching the 'bridging' role of the organisation between the individual and society at large. It fosters a certain mindset instead of providing strict guidelines for action. In drawing on the presented functionality taxonomy, the model serves to translate the vision internally so that employees can make sense of the context in which they do their work.

5.10 VandeMoortele

The management model applied by VandeMoortele is merely a mental construct or a vision on how labour relations can enhance the business strategy. It coherently outlines the way employees are involved in the organisation, in decision making processes and how the organisation enforced mutually dependent relations. The model seeks to translate a vision on human capital in order to meet the complex issues in the low cost high flexibility industry VandeMoortele acts.

5.11 Lloyds TSB

Lloyds TSB utilises the EFQM model in order to align the business strategy with the demands of a responsible organisation. The EFQM model supports the organisation in reflecting on its operations and policies through extended self-assessment possibilities. The EFQM model provides an holistic perspective integrating corporate social responsibility and the business strategy in order to

Table 1. Classifying the management models

Model functionality / Company	Translating	Monitoring	Understanding
Cilag			*
Henkel	*		
Danske Bank		*	*
Agrofair			
Gax du France		*	*
ABN AMRO Real Brazil	*		
Post Danmark	*	*	*
Water Corporation of Western Australia	*		
Triodos	*		
Bosch	*	*	
VandeMoortele	*		
NN			
Lloyds TSB	*	*	*

align value creation with the needs and expectations of a diverse set of stakeholders. Where the conventional quality models focus on the relation between customers and organisation, Lloyds TSB clearly moves forward to a societal perspective on its organisation. The EFQM model gives the organisation the handles to systematically reflect on how the organisation performs. Based on this monitoring functionality areas for improvement are identified. The model thus in first instance helps the organisation to reflect on its practices and in a second step to inform decisions on how to improve existing practices.

Taking a birds' eye view on the models in use by the companies it becomes apparent that the models appear in many shapes and sizes. Some are more elaborated then others, some are quantitative others qualitative. In figure 2. the models are characterised by their functionality.From this table it is easy to identify that the majority of the models aim to translate and visualise a vision for the future. These models are used to fuel interaction about the vision and how to put it into practice. Furthermore the model becomes an internal frame of reference through which actions of individuals are aligned to the organisation and the direction it goes. As such the models are becoming part of the collective mental framework through which organisational routines are embedded.

6   Trends and future developments

The chapters in this book show how 12 companies have established management models in order to cope with the complexities and dynamics within the organisation and the relations to the context in which the organisation operates. In all cases the models are different kind of answers to these developments in the context and the challenges they pose to the organisation. We will use the remainder of this chapter to have a closer look at what these models actually address. This is done by exploring the kind of goals that are envisioned and how they are 'translated'. In other words how the models seek to increase understanding for acting and subsequently what is being monitored.

6.1 Envisioned goals

When reviewing models that seek to translate a goal or vision, it becomes clear that all companies formulate goals that encompass a broad conception of the organisations' objective. The often referred to mantra that 'the business of business is to make a profit' does not seem to hold. ABN AMRO for example proclaims: "We need to influence capitalism to become more inclusive and humane". The social commitment of Henkel is in this regard is also illustrative: "We contribute to society through our brands and technologies that make peoples lives easier, better and more beautiful, while always striving to harmonize economic, ecological and social objectives". What the words of these companies show is that by using management models these phrases gradually become embedded into organizational action. Where statements easily can become empty promises, these cases demonstrate that a model helps to foster organizational commitment, understanding and develop a focus towards desired results. For the Triodos Bank, which has a firmly elaborated and rooted vision on sustainability, translating this vision serves to address the dilemmas between increasing economies of scale and professionalism versus sticking to the envisioned goals of social renewal. The Water Corporation of Western Australia used its business principles to start off a complete transformation of the organization.

6.2 Increasing understanding

Models that predominantly are used to increase specifically the understanding of managers that need to steer operations, are exceptional in this volume. Only Post Denmark, Danske Bank and Cilag use such models. The models used by Cilag are dynamic and mathematically founded. The models explicitly mimic real life decision situations. The models aim to increase learning to cope with increasingly complex situations. As an unforeseen side-effect the introduction of these models caused a shift in how decisions were made. Because the models enable to simulate decisions, they now can be based on a theory of action – or even a theory *in* action – in which proposed solutions can be tested. As a result decisions are better founded and more effective. The value chain model of Danske Bank supports managers in understanding the relation between employee satisfaction, customer loyalty and financial performance. By connecting these concept managers can adopt a holistic view on which they can base their decisions. The quantitative nature of the model convincingly shows how the concepts do affect one another. The model forms a robust instrument to increase the understanding of intangible assets within the bank. The integral excellence model used by Post Denmark gives a framework for managers to understand and interpret many processes and elements of the organisation. Adopting the model supported a fundamental transformation process within the organisation. It needed to transform from a bureaucratic semi-governmental organisation into a commercial business. The EFQM model was applied to facilitate this process, by offering guidance in this complex change processes. The model shows which elements and relations are relevant and provide a conceptual structure for initiating changing activities. All models that aim to support collective actions within the organisation have the quality of integrating and connecting a wide range of relevant elements. In doing so they present managers with a framework through which they not only can reduce the complexity but also of managing action.

6.3 Monitoring performance

Only three models are used to monitor how acting fosters the desired results. The EFQM models adopted by Lloyds TSB and Post Denmark are explicitly used to assess organisational performance. These assessments are conducted both internally as a self-assessment and externally through a benchmark against other organisations. The EFQM model provides the organisations a framework for making 'a picture' of the current state of performance of the organisation. The benefit of the model is that it facilitates shared understanding among managers of the elements and relations that affect the organisations' performance. The results of such an assessment enable to discuss the quality and causes of the current state and advance improvement actions based on a shared conceptual level of understanding. The value chain model of the Danske Bank is an instrument through which managers can monitor how actions in the area of human resource management affect customer loyalty and eventually financial performance. As a result, managers possess a monitoring instrument that demonstrates how effective certain actions are and how they contribute to the envisioned goals. Only a minority of the models support managers in monitoring the performance of the organisation. The models that do support this are to some extend quantifiable and relate several key elements of the organisation. By relating these elements in a quantifiable manner the models contribute to the understanding of managers of how different elements affect the performance of the organisation.

7 Concluding remarks

Organising and managing a business – creating value by transforming inputs into outputs – has become increasingly complex over the past decades. Contemporary business organisations face a pluralistic context that puts growing demands on the nature and its underlying processes of the value that is created. This implies that not only the actual value – expressed and measured not only in financial but also in ecological and social terms – that is being created needs to be monitored but also how this has come about. Transparency based on a clear vision and coherent set of goals seems to be the answer here. The number of stakeholders that put pressure on the organisation increases as well as the need for transparency through which organisational value creation processes become apparent inside and outside the organisation. Organisations must respond appropriately to these pressures in order to remain profitable in the short and the long term. They are requested to act responsive and responsible towards a wide array of stakeholders, some of which are known but some of which can present themselves at the doorstep of the organisation without being invited. On top of these new demands they are naturally asked to act flexible, be innovative and cost-competitive. These growing demands can be in conflict with each other at times. For the Water Corporation of Western Australia the dilemma raised how to maintain a business in water when water supplies becomes endangered. These kind of developments require from the organisation that they are able to respond fast and well informed; they need to be efficient and effective in their internal and boundary-spanning activities. Management models in this respect are instruments organisations utilise to support an array of organisational processes. As can be observed in the previous chapters, they play a role as unifying framework in order to create a shared understanding and platform for interaction and action. By using a model internal and external issues and developments are interpreted within a common framework. This way decisions can be made more coherent and thus effective and efficient. In this final chapter three main functionalities of models have been suggested: translating a vision, creating understanding and monitoring performance. In our view these functionalities support the key organisational processes of envisioning, acting and reflecting. Still, most models that are presented here serve one main functionality. In order for organisations to respond quickly and appropriately to external development it seems to be key to closely connect envisioning, acting and reflecting. Only if these processes are constantly in contact an organisation can respond quickly to changing expectations. If for example an organisation cannot monitor its performance, corrective actions might come to late. Models can support an organisation in learning, in envisioning how to connect these processes by integrating the functionalities of translating the vision, creating understanding and monitoring performance. These holistic models – such as for example the EFQM model deployed by Post Denmark and Lloyds TSB – create the framework that integrates the organisational processes.

In this chapter an interactionist's perspective was used to review the models. This perspective regards interaction as a fundamental quality of organisations. Since this is only one way of explaining models, other perspectives and theories can also be used. Guilen (1994) for example reviews models by introducing three basic perspectives on management: scientific management, human relations and structural analysis. He concentrates his classification on the technical task of management and the ideological aspect that frames authority relations. Zbaracki (1998) elaborates on the differences between the rhetoric versus the technical execution of total quality management. Models are in this view conceptualised as part of the rhetoric managers use. Furthermore an institutional perspective can be used to explore if organisation tend to use the same models in a certain industry (DiMaggio and Powell, 1983). This theoretical perspective also distinguishes between the symbolic use of management models as fads and fashion and the actual use in practice (Abrahamson and Fairchild, 1999). What can be concluded here is that a variety of theories of management and organisations can be used in order to explore and explain the concept of management models. This chapter introduced an interactionist perspective as a first attempt to explore management models from a different perspective. It is evident that this perspective depicts only a restricted picture. Further research employing multiple theoretical and conceptual frameworks can advance our understanding of what management models are and what their role and functionality is within organisations.

References

Ambrahamson, E. and G. Fairchild (1999) Management Fashion: Lifecycles, Triggers, and Collective Learning, *Administrative Science Quarterly*, Vol. 44, No. 4, pp. 708-740

DiMaggio, P.J, and W.W. Powell (1983) The Iron Cage Revisited: Institutional Isomorphism and Collective Rationality in Organizational Fields, *American Sociological Review*, Vol. 48, No.2, pp. 147-160

Guillen, M.F. (1994) The age of Eclecticism: Current Organizational Trends and the Evolution of Management Models, *Sloan Management Review*, Vol 36, no. 1, pp. 75-86

Zbaracki, M. (1998) The Rhetoric and Reality of Total Quality Management, *Administrative Science Quarterly*, Vol. 43, No. 3, pp. 602-636

About the Authors

Nikos Avlonas is a founder and Managing Director of the Centre for Sustainability & Excellence (CSE) – a global think tank and sustainable development solutions advisory network – based in Athens with offices in Brussels and Dubai. He is also a part-time Professor at the American College Of Greece (Deree College) teaching, since 2000, Corporate Social Responsibility, Total Quality Management, and Supply Chain Management. He specialises in sustainability, CSR, governance, business ethics, change and performance management. He has carried out numerous projects in leading organisations including Fortune Global 500 companies. He has cooperated as project expert with major European organisations including Siemens, TNT, ORACLE ,Lloyds TSB, and BT in the development of European Foundation for Quality Management (EFQM) CSR Framework and relevant tools and methodologies. Additionally he participated as an expert in the EFQM Excellence Model Executive Review Committee, which produced the Business Excellence Model (2003 edition).

Contact details: avlonas@cse-net.org

Kai von Bargen is Head of Corporate Affairs & Sponsoring at Henkel and responsible for Corporate Citizenship Communication. With his team he coordinates various projects concerning Corporate Citizenship and Sponsoring and communicates relevant information to the media and other stakeholders. Prior to joining Henkel, Kai worked 15 years as a journalist for various newspapers, agencies and radio stations also acting as consultant for the Dortmund-based Deutsche Hörfunkakademie for eight years. Since 2006 he has been teaching Corporate Social Responsibility at the University of Applied Sciences in Gelsenkirchen.

Contact details: Kai.vonbargen@henkel.com

Birgit Benkhoff is a professor of Human Resource Management at Technische Universität Dresden. She received her BSc in Economics and her MSc in Industrial Relations and Personnel Management as well as her PhD at the London School of Economics and Political Science. Her main research interest are flexible employment contracts and flexible forms of organizations/virtual organizations. Another of her current projects deals with the management of health and safety policies.

Contact details: Birgit.Benkhoff@tu-dresden.de

Peter Blom (Leiden, 1956) studied economics at the Vrije Universiteit Amsterdam from 1975 until 1979. He has been with Triodos Bank since it was founded in 1980. He is now the CEO and Chairman of the Executive Board. Prior to become CEO and Chairman in 1997, he was joint Managing Director and appointed in that position in December 1988. Prior to this he was a senior account manager business banking for the bank. He was also co-founder and Chairman of the International Association of Investors in the Social Economy (INAISE) in 1988 and a co-founder of the Social Venture Network Europe.

Contact details: peter.blom@triodos.nl

Dave Boselie conducted PhD research on agricultural market reforms in Vietnam from 1994-98. From 1998 until 2003 he worked as consultant in international supply chain projects at the Agricultural Economics Research Institute in the Hague. These projects focussed on the development of new supplier relationships for perishable products in retail driven supply chains in Asia and Africa. Currently he is managing director of AgroFair Assistance & Development Foundation (AFAD) which is closely affiliated with AgroFair Europe BV, a producer co-owned trade company that specializes in fair-trade and organic certified fruits. AFAD supports the development of producer organizations so that they can gain market access and continue to meet the increasing quality standards of (super)markets.

Contact details: dave.boselie@agrofair.nl

Christa Büchler is Human Resources Manager at Henkel and has been involved in the Company's Corporate Citizenship for more than 15 years. All components of Corporate Citizenship at Henkel are coordinated under the umbrella of the Henkel Smile brand. Christa is responsible for the areas of Corporate Donations focusing on Henkel activities and sites. Moreover, she is coordinator of the Corporate Volunteering program at Henkel, known as MIT Initiative, the Henkel Friendship Initiative e.V. for disaster relief aid throughout the world and of long term projects.

Contact details: Christa.Buechler@henkel.com

Vincent Dufour is presently working as HR International Project Manager at Gaz de France Headquarters in Paris. He is involved in the building of international HR policies and guidelines for the group. From July 2003 to November 2006, he was director of Human Resources and Communication of a 400-employee establishment based in the centre of France, in charge of gas and electricity local distribution network and jointly owned by Gaz de France and EDF. He has been Member of the Prospective Committee on 2005 key technologies of the French Ministry of Industry and working in EDF as Head of an economic expertise unit on international projects (1996-2000). He has multicultural experience due to regular contacts with large international companies and due to previous expatriations in Italy (1992-1994), Nordic Countries (1994-1996) and Japan (2001-2003).

Contact details: vincent.dufour@gazdefrance.com

Jacob Eskildsen is associate professor and a member of the Centre for Corporate Performance at The Aarhus School of Business. Before entering academia Jacob worked as quality manager in a Danish subsidiary of a large multinational company. He holds an MSc and a PhD from the Aarhus School of Business. He is the author of over 75 publications in journals and books. He is in charge of "The Danish Customer Satisfaction Index" which is the Danish platform of the ESPSI Rating initiative. Jacob is also a member of the research projects, "The Danish Excellence Index" and "The European Employee Index©". As part of his research he has been involved in a number of studies in individual companies, trying to identify the relationship between the intangible assets of the company, such as customer and employee satisfaction with financial performance. Additionally, he is in charge of the masters' programme on Business Performance Management at the Aarhus School of Business.

Contact details: eskildsen@asb.dk

Robert Humphries is a systems ecologist with interests in the behaviour and management of complex systems. He has worked as a university research fellow, as an environmental consultant, and in research and policy roles in the Western Australian Environmental Protection Authority and the Australian water industry. His work and personal interests have taken him to all Australian states and several other countries. He was born and educated in Perth, Western Australia, and studied Zoology and Botany at the University of Western Australia. He received his doctorate in Environmental Biology at the Australian National University, Canberra, in 1980. Bob has worked on the restoration of degraded catchments and waterways for much of his career, and on the successful restoration the nutrient-enriched Peel-Harvey Estuary south of Perth. Bob has worked with the WA Water Corporation since 1996, firstly as Environment Manager and since June 2004 as Manager Sustainability.

Contact details: Bob.Humphries@WaterCorporation.com.au

Matej Janovjak is director of the Department of *Strategic Process Management & Methods* at GPSG EMEA of Johnson & Johnson. His very wide industrial activities, mainly based in Pharma and the paper-making industry, have been focused on process and project engineering, industrial manufacturing, facility master planning, process-related organisational design and strategy development and deployment. In his several functions as engineering and production manager as well as Member of the Board of Directors he has been introducing and applying, among others, a wide spectrum of advanced modelling and simulation methods on strategic, tactical and operational levels. He has lectured on control systems at the University of Applied Science, Muttenz, Basle, for more than 25 years.

Contact details: mjanovja@cilch.jnj.com

Anders Jeppesen, Head of TQM and Strategy, Post Denmark A/S, has worked with different aspects of quality through most of his 20 years with Post Denmark. He has been responsible for utilising the Excellence Model in the company since implementation in 1998. Today his area also covers strategy, organisational development, process management and benchmarking.

Jan Jonker is associate professor at the Nijmegen School of Management (NSM) of the Radboud University Nijmegen [RUN – Holland]. His research interest lies at the crossroads of management and corporate social responsibility, in particular in relation to the development of business strategy and value creation. He holds an MSc from Leiden University and a PhD from Nijmegen University. He has written so far 17 books alone or with others and published over 120 articles. He is a member of the editorial board of several journals. He has been (and is) a member of numerous scientific conference committee. Besides his academic activities he also has been a business consultant for the past fifteen years. Having started off with projects related to organisational diagnosis and -change, his focus has (dramatically) changed and has become concentrated on CSR and Business Strategy during recent years. He now works not only in the Netherlands but also for international clients in Europe.

Contact details: Janjonker@wxs.nl

Robert Kinnell is a Senior Manager at Ernst & Young in Perth where he leads the Sustainability Advisory team. Bob has advised some of Western Australia's largest companies and government agencies in assisting them to understand the value proposition around a sustainable development focus to major capital projects and operational strategy. Bob's career has taken him from the UK to the Atacama Desert of Chile and Peru where he worked as a hydrogeologist developing water resources for the Copper mining industry to Buenos Aires, Argentina where he introduced new wastewater treatment technologies to the winery and intensive livestock industries. Since his return to Australia in 2002 Bob has been involved in the development of the WA state sustainability strategy, is the author of several papers on sustainable development related topics and has presented at Committee for Economic Development of Australia, the Property Council and other public conferences and forums. Bob is a member of the board of management for **Institute for** Sustainability and Technology Policy at Murdoch University, the environment management committee of the Chamber of Commerce and Industry WA, the fundamental pressures working group for the WA State of the Environment report 2006 and is a Director of Community Vision Inc.

Contact details: Bob.Kinnell@watercorporation.com.au

Kai Kristensen is full professor of applied statistics and a member of the Centre for Corporate Performance at the Aarhus School of Business. He is the author of several books and more than 100 articles in Scandinavian and international journals. He is co-founder of the Danish Quality Award and he serves on the prize committee for both the Danish Quality Award and the Public Sector Quality Award. He is one of the founding fathers of the European Customer Satisfaction Program and he is director of research of the International Foundation for Customer Focus.

Jeroen Kroezen is CEO of AGrofair Europe B.V. since 2003. In this position he is responsible for the holding and subsidiaries of Agrofair, aiming at strong growth through diversification of products and markets. He finished Msc in Economics from the University of Amsterdam with a specialization in development and corporate economics. He started at Agrofair in 2001 as general director of Agrofair Benelux. Before joining Agrofair he held the positions of advisor international trade and advisor economic affairs at SNV Equador from 1996-2001. Before that he worked as logistical and financial employee at Memisa Medicus Mundi. In this position he was mainly working in Africa.

Contact details: Jeroen.kroezen@agrofair.nl

René Leegte is Chief Commercial Officer for AgoFair Europe bv. Since April 2006. After his study Economics of Development at the Agricultural University of Wageningen, he worked as personal secretary of mr. drs. F. Bolkestein, then leader of the Dutch liberal Party VVD. After 4 years, he joined Unilevers' business unit IgloMora in the marketing – sales discipline. He started to work for 'Mora' and moved to 'Ola' to become responsible for the power brands Magnum, Cornetto and Solero. As he was looking for challenges to make a difference in social corporate sustainability, he joined DHV sustainable consultancy in Amersfoort. He gave an impulse in the development of the business unit and facilitated and implemented sustainable strategy in several (listed) companies. Being CCO is combining all skills and competences learned in past positions. In his current position he is responsible for the development and implementation of AgroFairs' commercial strategy. AgroFairs' 5 national offices report directly to him. René – among others – subscribed the imitative of an open letter by the so called 'leaders for Nature' to the parliament aiming for attention on climate change and sustainability.

Contact details: rene.leegte@planet.nl

Helmut Lutzmann is plant manager at Vandemoortele Deutschland GmbH und responsible for employee development in Dresden and in the German plants of the Vandemoortele group. During the last ten years he has worked on the development of new management methods in cooperation with external partners.

Contact details: Helmut.Lutzmann@vandemoortele.com

Lars S. Mørch, Senior Executive Vice President, Head of Human Resources Danske Bank Group.

Nicole Pettit is the Education Consultant for the Water Corporation's Sustainability Strategy and is responsible for planning and implementing the Corporation's learning and development program for sustainability. Born and educated in Perth, Nicole graduated from Curtin University in Western Australia with a Bachelor of Education and has recently completed a Masters of Business Administration. Nicole has many years experience in a range of organisational development and community education roles. This experience includes working at the Western Australian Chamber of Minerals and Energy to provide education and training advice to the mining, oil and gas sectors, the Western Australian Department of Environmental Protection to develop and implement community environmental education programs and as a teacher in Indigenous communities in the vast Pilbara Region of Western Australia.

Contact details: Nicole.Pettit@watercorporation.com.au

Michel van Pijkeren is a young faculty member at the Nijmegen School of Management. He holds an MSc in International Management. Since graduation he has published several articles and collaborated on chapters concerning CSR and quality management. At present he is developing a PhD research project concerning the strategic significance of CSR, focusing on the issue of multiple value creation in relation to management models. Since 2005 he has been working as editorial assistant on two volumes on Corporate Social Responsibility (CSR): "The Challenge of Organizing and Implementing CSR" (Palgrave 2006) and "Management Models for CSR" (Springer, 2006). Additionally, he acted in the same role on 'Management Models for the Future' by Jonker and Eskildsen (Springer, 2007, forthcoming). He is also employed as a quality manager at the Bosch Communication Center (The Netherlands).

Contact details: mvanpijkeren@hotmail.com

Natalie Reilly has a background in economics, accounting and strategic planning. The first 12 years of her career were spent in the areas of accounting and taxation, working for Coopers and Lybrand, a chartered accounting firm and GIO Australia Limited in Sydney. On returning to Perth in 1997, Natalie began life in the Water Corporation in the Finance Division and then spent several years in the Strategic Business Performance unit of the Corporation at a time when the organisation was experiencing a significant shift in its business drivers, such as climate change and changing community expectations. As a result the need for "Sustainable management of water services" became the focus for the organisation and Natalie was appointed as the founding member of the Water Corporation's Sustainability team (now expanded to five) and mandated to integrate Sustainability practices, policies and thinking throughout the organisation. Contact details: Natalie.Reilly@WaterCorporation.com.au

Christine Schneider is Sustainability Reporting & Stakeholder Dialogue Manager at Henkel. Since joining Henkel in 2003, she has been responsible for Henkel's Safety, Health and Environment Reporting, Sustainability Ratings as well as internal and external dialogue on sustainability issues. Christine graduated as an engineer from the Technical University Berlin in 1994. Since then, she has been involved in a wide range of environmental and sustainability reporting projects. Prior to joining Henkel, she worked as Market Researcher and Consultant at KPMG, a major international accounting firm, as an environmental verifier and auditor according to ISO 14001.
Contact details: Christine.schneider@henkel.com

Christel Scholten is a manager of the Sustainable Development Department of ABN AMRO Real in Brazil. She joined the team in 2003 after working at the head office in Amsterdam for two years. She is responsible for integrating sustainable development into various aspects of the organisation, from strategy and governance to policies, processes and educational programs. Christel is Canadian and has lived in several other countries including Mexico, The Netherlands and Bangladesh where she spent time working in the area of Microfinance with organisations such as the Grameen Bank and BRAC. She has a Bachelor of Commerce from the University of Saskatchewan, Canada and a Master of Science in Responsibility and Business Practice from the University of Bath, UK. She was very involved in the international youth organisation, AIESEC, is an active member of Pioneers of Change and serves on the board of The Shire, a learning centre in Canada for the study and practice of how to build a sustainable human future.
Contact details: christel.scholten@br.abnamro.com

Jan-Dirk Seiler-Hausmann is R&D and Sustainability Communications Manager at Henkel. Since joining Henkel in 2002, he has been responsible for R&D and Sustainability Communications. Jan-Dirk graduated in political sciences from Freie Universität Berlin in 1994. Since then, he has been involved in the topics of climate change and sustainable development. Prior to joining Henkel, he worked at the German Federal Environmental Ministry and at the Wuppertal Institute for Climate, Environment and Energy. Together with Ernst U. von Weisäcker he edited two collections of essays on eco-efficiency (*Ökoeffizienz: Mangement der Zukunft* and *Eco-efficiency and Beyond*).

Contact details: Jan-Dirk.Seiler-Hausmann@henkel.com

Henrik D. Sørensen, CEO Ennova A/S.

John Swannick is an issues management and stakeholder relations specialist for Lloyds TSB. His brief includes work in public policy, corporate governance, business ethics, reputational risk, investor relations, community engagement, employee development and change management. In this role, he has been instrumental in the development and implementation of Lloyds TSB's Group Code of Business Conduct and social and environmental reporting. He developed the framework for Lloyds TSB's Corporate Responsibility steering committee of senior executives who oversee policy and strategy across the business. He was a member of the European Foundation for Quality Management working group which developed the EFQM CSR Framework. He is an economics graduate of the University of Bath and a Fellow of the Royal Society of Arts.

Contact details: John.Swannick@LloydsTSB.co.uk

Markus Schwaninger is professor of management at the University of St. Gallen, Switzerland. His research is focused on the study of complex sociotechnical systems, with a methodological focus on organisational cybernetics and system dynamics. His research projects to date have been related to organisational intelligence, the design, transformation and learning of organisations, and to systemic issues of sustainability. Schwaninger is the author of roughly 190 publications in six languages, including *Organizational Transformation and Learning* (Wiley, 1996; with Espejo and Schuhmann), and *Intelligent Organizations* (Springer, 2006). He has lectured widely, on four continents, and is involved in international, transdisciplinary research projects.

Contact details: markus.schwaninger@unisg.ch

William Varey is the Principal of *Forsyth Consulting Group*, a strategic management consultancy that specializes in the development of organizational and public sector sustainability strategies and the dynamics of social systems psychology impacting on societal change. He has qualifications in public international and commercial law, business management, organisational psychology and integral post-metaphysics. His main area of research and practice is in the evolutionary emergence of human social systems. He is a member of the Association for Humanistic Psychology and is an Associate Fellow of the Australian Institute of Management.

Contact details: william@fcg.com.au

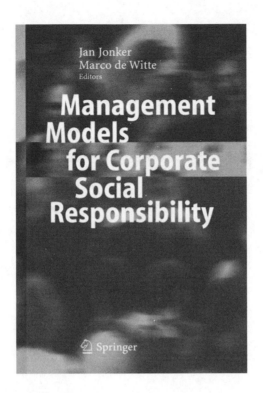

Jonker, Jan; Witte, Marco de (Eds.):

Management Models for Corporate Social Responsibility

2006, X, 378 p. 57 illus., Hardcover
ISBN: 978-3-540-33246-6

In recent years the field of Corporate Social Responsibility (CSR) has impressively progressed. This has resulted in a number of tried and tested management models - models that have demonstrated added value in everyday organisational practice. This book harvests this experience leading to an accessible and readable volume with an overview of those models in a hands-on manner. In total more than forty models from around the world are brought together. Each contribution is structured around one central figure while describing concisely the nature, the use, actual experiences and some do's and don'ts of CSR. The book is written for a managerial and consultants audience, people that have to deal with CSR in everyday practice.